Interpretationshilfen

Crooked Letter, Crooked Letter

Tom Franklin

W0240010

Cornelsen

Crooked Letter, Crooked Letter · Interpretationshilfe

Erarbeitet von Paul Maloney

Verlagsredaktion
Neil Porter, Martina Krause (Bildrechte)

Umschlagdesign
Heike Börner, orangerie grafikdesign

Technische Umsetzung
L101 Mediengestaltung, Fürstenwalde

www.cornelsen.de

1. Auflage, 1. Druck 2017

© 2017 Cornelsen Verlag GmbH, Berlin

Das Werk und seine Teile sind urheberrechtlich geschützt.
Jede Nutzung in anderen als den gesetzlich zugelassenen Fällen bedarf der vorherigen schriftlichen Einwilligung des Verlages.
Hinweis zu den §§ 46, 52 a UrhG: Weder das Werk noch seine Teile dürfen ohne eine solche Einwilligung eingescannt und in ein Netzwerk eingestellt oder sonst öffentlich zugänglich gemacht werden.
Dies gilt auch für Intranets von Schulen und sonstigen Bildungseinrichtungen.

Druck: AZ Druck und Datentechnik GmbH, Kempten

ISBN 978-3-06-035502-0

PEFC/04-31-2260

PEFC zertifiziert
Dieses Produkt stammt aus nachhaltig bewirtschafteten Wäldern und kontrollierten Quellen.

www.pefc.de

Contents

All page and line numbers in this book refer to the Cornelsen edition of the novel (ISBN 978-3-06-035438-2), with the exception of cross-references to other sections of this book.

To the student

While an *Interpretationshilfe* can never replace your own reading of the novel, it can help give you a better understanding of the novel. Of course, most authors expect their readers to be able to understand (and enjoy!) their works without holding a study guide in one hand and the novel in the other. Tom Franklin is no exception. But keep in mind that Franklin wrote his novel for American readers, who, as a rule, are familiar with most of the things the author alludes to. For a German reader, some aspects of the story might seem a bit strange (like the connection between sports and university study). That is one of the reasons why this study guide was written. Moreover, the story is set in a region of the USA that has its own unique history and culture, a region that even many Americans are unfamiliar with. In this study guide, you will therefore find the background information on the Deep South, its history and culture, that you need to understand the novel.

In some ways *Crooked Letter, Crooked Letter* is challenging, even for experienced readers. Both the chronology and the point of view jump back and forth, from present to past and from one character to another. In this study guide, you will find:

- concise summaries of the plot
- schematic overviews that enable you to pinpoint the events of the novel
- information on the characters, the narrative structure, the imagery, the themes and the genre of the novel
- a written test, together with a step-by-step analysis of the given tasks.

The Author

Thomas Gerald Franklin (usually just Tom Franklin) was born in Dickinson, Alabama on July 7, 1963. Dickinson, a tiny hamlet in southwest Alabama with a population of less than 500, was presumably the real-life model for Chabot, Mississippi, in the novel *Crooked Letter, Crooked Letter*. Franklin moved with his family in 1981 to Mobile, Alabama, where he attended the University of South Alabama, graduating with a Bachelor of Arts in English. While attending college, Franklin supported himself with part-time jobs in heavy industry, the chemical industry and in a hospital morgue. His job experiences sharpened his vision for the details of ordinary life. He later attended the University of Arizona, where he graduated with a Master of Fine Arts in Fiction in 1998. Franklin has taught writing classes at a number of colleges and universities.

Franklin's first published work of fiction, a collection of short stories that appeared as *Poachers* in 1998, won the Edgar Allan Poe Award for Best Mystery Story (for the title story). His first novel, *Hell at the Breech*, followed in 2003; a second novel, *Smonk*, appeared in 2006. His most successful novel to date has been *Crooked Letter, Crooked Letter* (2010), for which he received the Crime Writers' Association Gold Dagger Award. Franklin also co-authored the novel *The Tilted World* (2013) with his wife, the poet Beth Ann Fennelly.

All of Franklin's fiction is set in the Deep South and is rooted in rural southern history and culture. The tension between the traditional southern lifestyle (hunting and fishing, segregation, patriarchal family structures) and modern American society forms the substrate from which his stories evolve. While some critics regard Franklin mainly as a crime writer, his broad realism and keen moral sense place him in the context of other southern writers such as Flannery O'Connor and Cormac McCarthy.

Synopsis

The events of the plot center on the small logging town of Chabot, Mississippi. In the mid-1960s, a young black woman named Alice Jones worked as a housemaid for a white couple, Carl and Ina Ott. Shortly after the birth of their first and only child, Larry, Alice became pregnant and had to leave the Otts' house. Later in the novel Carl Ott, now dead, is revealed to be the father. Alice moves to Chicago, where she gives birth to a son, Silas. When Silas is 14, circumstances force Alice to flee from Chicago with her son and return to Chabot, where she lives in a primitive log cabin belonging to the Otts. The Otts' son Larry, a shy, bookish boy treated contemptuously by his father, befriends Silas, not knowing that they are half-brothers. Their friendship is rather one-sided and exists only outside of school, where Larry is an outsider and Silas a popular baseball player. The friendship ends abruptly when Silas refuses to return a rifle Larry borrowed from his father and, in a subsequent fight organized by Carl Ott, Larry calls Silas a 'nigger'.

Larry's life changes dramatically when a teenage girl mysteriously disappears after supposedly going out on a date with him. Larry tells the police that the girl, Cindy Walker, in reality only used him to meet secretly with her boyfriend, and that he never saw her again after dropping her off outside of town. Later in the novel, we learn that her boyfriend was Silas. As Cindy's body is never found, the criminal charges against Larry are dropped, but everyone in Chabot is convinced that he killed her. Later, Larry's father dies in a car accident, his mother has to be moved to a nursing home, and Larry lives alone in his empty house with little or no contact with the outside world, ostracized by the community.

Twenty-five years after Cindy's disappearance, Silas, who left for Oxford (Mississippi), where he finished high school and attended college, has returned to Chabot as police constable. Tina Rutherford, the teenage daughter of the owner of the local sawmill, has disappeared, and everyone is sure that 'Scary Larry' has found another victim. While investigating the death of a suspected drug dealer, Silas uncovers signs that his former childhood friend may be in trouble. Then Larry is found lying on the floor of his house, a bullet wound in his chest. He is taken to hospital and falls in a coma after emergency surgery. Silas, convinced of Larry's innocence, looks for clues pointing to the real killer, but instead finds Tina's body buried in the ground beneath the old cabin where he once lived with his mother. A young white woman calls Silas's attention to a man named Wallace Stringfellow, who befriended Larry a few months before the girl disappeared. When Silas comes to Stringfellow's house to question him, a gunfight ensues, in the course of which both men are injured. Stringfellow commits suicide while fleeing from the police, and Silas wakes up in a hospital bed next to Larry. Larry at first rejects Silas's attempts at reconciliation, but in the end the two men, who now admit that they are half-brothers, make their peace with each other.

Timeline of Events

With the exception of 1979 and 1982, all given dates are approximate and are intended only as an aid to understanding the chronology of the novel.

when	what
1965	Larry Ott is born. Alice Jones becomes pregnant and moves to Chicago, where her son Silas is born.
1979	Alice and Silas move back to Chabot. Larry and Silas attend Chabot Middle School. Larry and Silas become friends outside of school until (in June) their father forces them to fight. Alice moves with Silas to Fulsom, where he attends high school (as does Larry).

1982	Silas has a secret affair with Cindy Walker until she disappears. Larry drops out of school. Silas leaves Fulsom for a high school in Oxford, Mississippi.
↑	Silas attends the University of Mississippi; later he goes to a police academy.
	Larry joins the army and becomes a mechanic.
	Carl Ott is killed in a car accident. Larry quits the army and returns to Chabot, where he takes over his father's garage.
↓	Larry frightens off a boy who has been breaking into his barn.
1997	Ina Ott is moved to a nursing home.
1999	Alice Jones dies.
2005	Silas Jones returns to Chabot as town constable.
2006	Wallace Stringfellow begins visiting Larry.
2007	Stringfellow stops visiting Larry.
Sept. 2007	Tina Rutherford is reported missing.
one week later	Stringfellow comes to Larry in the night (Sunday/Monday) and confesses that he has 'done something'.
Monday morning	Larry, worried about Stringfellow, tries in vain to reach Silas on the phone.

Tuesday	Silas finds the corpse of Morton Morrisette in a swamp. Larry is shot by Stringfellow (around noon). Silas drives to a white neighborhood where someone has put a rattlesnake in a mailbox. He phones his girlfriend Angie, an EMT, and asks her to check out Larry Ott's house. Angie finds Larry and has him taken to hospital.
Wednesday	Silas discovers Tina Rutherford's grave in the old hunting cabin.
Monday of the following week	Silas tells Angie the truth about his affair with Cindy Walker.
Tuesday	Silas learns that Larry has regained consciousness. He comes to the hospital and tells Larry and French about his involvement with Cindy.
later (same day?)	Silas goes back to the hospital and tries unsuccessfully to get Larry to tell him why he phoned him on Monday before the shooting. That evening, Silas meets Irina (a white woman who had a rattlesnake put in her mailbox) by chance in a bar. She tells him about a girlfriend who was nearly raped by Stringfellow.
the next day	Silas goes out to Stringfellow's house; a gunfight follows. Silas is badly injured, Stringfellow flees, commits suicide.
one day later	Larry tells French why he believes that Stringfellow murdered Tina Rutherford and shot him. Silas is wheeled into his room.
two days later	Silas is released from hospital.
12 days after the shooting	Larry leaves the hospital on his own. Silas finds him and drives him home.

Chapter Summaries

Chapter One

Summary: The first chapter of the novel consists mostly of exposition giving the reader background information on Larry Ott, one of the two main characters. It also contains an important plot element: the shooting of Larry Ott by a masked assailant.

The narrator describes what normally would have been a typical day in Larry's life. We learn that he is 41 years old, single, lives alone in the house he grew up in, that his mother is in a nursing home and his father presumably dead, that Larry works as a car mechanic at his own garage , where he has very few customers. He lives in a very isolated area and evidently has only one friend, a man named Wallace Stringfellow.

exposition: Larry Ott's life

We also find out that Larry is the suspect in a crime due to his past. The teenage daughter of the Rutherfords, owners of the sawmill in Chabot, has been missing for eight days, and Chief Inspector French visited Larry a

Larry: a suspicious character?

day earlier to search his house for clues. We also learn that Larry is not allowed to own a gun *'because of his past'* (p. 11, ll. 10 f.) and that his actions are closely watched by the local police (p. 12, l. 20 f.).

When Larry stops at his house to fetch a photo album before driving to the nursing home to visit his mother, he finds an armed assailant waiting for him in the living

room. The man is wearing a zombie mask that belongs to Larry. He says to him, *'Ever body knows what you did,'* (p. 13, ll. 24 f.), then fires a pistol at Larry's chest. Larry falls to the floor and loses consciousness. When he comes to, the assailant is still standing there, waiting for him to die.

Commentary: Notice how the author grabs the reader's attention with the very first sentence: *'The Rutherford girl had been missing for eight days when Larry Ott returned home and found a monster waiting in his house.'* This well-known literary technique is employed here so blatantly that it almost borders on parody. The author also uses a technique known as *in medias res*, meaning '(jumping) into the middle of things'. There is no introduction to the world of the novel; instead, we are confronted with disturbing, disconnected facts that we, the readers, must somehow make sense of.

grabbing the reader's attention

The opening chapter contains a number of details that all contribute to the impression that Larry is a loner and an outsider in the community:

interpreting the details

- the isolated location of his house,
- his lack of social contacts,
- his derelict roadside garage that no one ever stops at,

- his conversations with the chickens (suggesting they are all the company he has).

The hints in the first part of the chapter suggesting that Larry is under permanent police surveillance reinforce the feeling that this strange, solitary man may have something to hide.

two similar crimes

Two similar crimes separated by 25 years are alluded to in the first chapter. In each case, a teenage girl from the town (first Cindy Walker, later Tina Rutherford) disappeared under mysterious circumstances. In his thoughts, Larry is prepared to deny responsibility for both abductions (p. 13, ll. 28 f.), whereas his assailant seems to be convinced of his guilt (p. 13, ll. 24 f.). Possibly the stranger has come to seek revenge – but we should be careful about jumping to conclusions, as he might have a completely different motive.

questions to ask about the assailant

In a crime story, details can be extremely important. It is therefore necessary to pay attention to information that may seem irrelevant at first glance:

- Take the zombie mask, for instance: Larry recognizes the mask as one belonging to him. The mask was hidden in his house – so well hidden, that not even CI French found it. What does that tell us about the assailant?
- Another point is the assailant's behavior: he fires a shot point-blank into Larry's chest, then waits impatiently for Larry to die. Even when it becomes apparent that Larry may not die immediately from his chest wound, the masked assailant doesn't fire a second shot. What reason might he have for this? And why does he bother with the mask, if his only witness is not meant to survive?

Points to remember:

- Larry Ott is an outsider in Chabot.
- Twenty-five years after Cindy Walker's disappearance, another teenage girl has apparently been abducted.
- In the public mind, Larry Ott is evidently linked with the two disappearances.
- Someone (whose identity is unknown) wants Larry to die.

Chapter Two

Summary: The second chapter relates further incidents of the same day, but this time from the point of view of Silas Jones, the constable of Chabot.

At the beginning of the chapter, Silas is driving back from patrol duty when he observes buzzards circling in the sky. Thinking they might be attracted by the smell of a corpse, he drives into a swampy woodland area and walks alongside a creek until he finds the badly decayed body of Morton Morrisette, a former classmate and small-time drug dealer who – the police assume – was shot in his house a short time before. Silas notifies CI French and the emergency medical technicians (EMTs) and waits at the site until they arrive.

Silas Jones discovers a murder victim.

Later at the Chabot Town Hall Silas learns from French that Larry Ott's garage was closed when French drove past that morning. Silas is disturbed, as Larry has never failed to open and close punctually, in spite of his lack of business. When he is back on patrol that afternoon, he receives a radio message sending him to a poor white neighborhood where a rattlesnake has been discovered in a mailbox. Silas, still thinking about Larry, phones his girlfriend Angie, an EMT, and asks her to drive past the Otts' house. Silas drives over and kills the snake. The young women who live there are certain that someone put the snake in their mailbox to kill one of them, but

Silas worries about Larry.

have no idea who it could be. While Silas is driving back to town, he receives a call from Angie, who has evidently found Larry severely wounded in his house.

background information

Commentary: In addition to the events of the plot, Chapter Two contains background information on the town of Chabot and on Silas Jones.

Chabot

We learn the following about Chabot:

- It has about five hundred inhabitants.
- It's completely dependent on the Rutherford sawmill, the major source of employment in the region.
- The Rutherfords are the largest landowners in the area.
- The town is run on a shoestring budget and in general makes an impoverished impression.
- Silas is the only police officer, sharing the Town Hall with the town clerk and a part-time mayor.

Silas

We learn the following about Silas:

- He left the town 25 years before to finish high school in Oxford.
- He attended the University of Mississippi, where he ruined his left arm playing baseball.

- After graduating, he enlisted in the Navy, then did police training before joining the college police in Oxford.
- Two years before the story begins, he applied for the position of town constable in Chabot.
- We also learn that Larry Ott attempted to contact Silas after the latter returned to Chabot, but Silas showed no interest.

Silas and Larry as protagonists

The first two chapters establish Larry Ott and Silas Jones as the protagonists of the plot. At first sight, they appear to be opposites:

- Larry is a crime suspect (and victim), Silas a police officer.
- Larry is a recluse with no social contacts, Silas a respected member of the community with an extended social network of colleagues and (former) girlfriends.

The fact that Larry attempted to contact Silas after his return to Chabot appears at first glance somewhat mysterious, hinting as it does at some past connection that has yet be established.

Chapter Three

flashback: Silas and his mother back in Chabot (1979)

Summary: Chapter Three consists of a flashback to the year 1979, when Silas and Larry, both 14 years old, meet for the first time. While Carl Ott is driving his son to school, he passes Alice Jones and her son standing by the side of the road in the freezing cold and offers them a ride. This pattern continues until Mrs. Ott, who has learned from Larry about the new passengers, takes matters into her own hands and drives Larry to school one morning. Instead of giving Silas and his mother a lift, she hands them second-hand winter coats and leaves them standing there.

Larry, now in the eighth grade, goes to a school where white pupils are in the minority. Awkward and untalented at sports, Larry has no white friends and is bullied by his black classmates. Silas, on the other hand, soon makes friends at school. The two boys have no contact until one day later that year, when Larry borrows one of his father's rifles and goes hunting. He meets Silas by chance near the log cabin where Silas and his mother still live. Larry shows Silas how to use a rifle and allows him to borrow it for a time.

Larry's social status at school

Larry and Silas become friends

Commentary: The third chapter throws light on the relationships within the Ott family while hinting at the connection between the Otts and the Joneses. Carl Ott appears to live a double life: at home strict and uncommunicative, at work talkative and good-natured, the center of a crowd of like-minded men. Apparently, he lives a double life in another sense as well, as his wife immediately becomes suspicious when she hears about the two new passengers in his truck. Later, we learn the cause of her distrust: her husband was having an affair with their black housemaid, Alice Jones, while she was pregnant with Larry, and now Alice is back again with her and Carl's son, Silas.

Larry's parents – a strained relationship

Larry: a born loner

We also gain further insight into the roots of Larry's loneliness. Larry is – to his knowledge – an only child, he has no friends at school, and his one-sided interest in horror fiction makes him an outsider. Larry's only attempt at gaining the recognition of his white classmates ends in disaster. Larry sees himself as having inherited his mother's feminine looks and temperament; his father seems to feel only contempt for the son who is so different from him and bans him from his place of work until Larry is twelve. Caught between attachment to his mother and fear of his father, Larry – probably unthinkingly – reveals his father's secret to his mother, which abruptly ends the arrangement, leads to new tension between husband and wife, and leaves Larry with the vague feeling that he has '*betrayed a trust between himself and his father*' (p. 48, l. 17).

Larry is described as a victim of '*redistricting*' (p. 46, l. 4), meaning that the boundaries of the school districts were changed so that he had to go to Chabot Middle School, where whites were in the minority (even today, there are regions in Mississippi where African Americans form the majority). Middle school in the USA comprises grades 6–8. The incident that Larry recalls here (p. 57, ll. 19 ff.) is significant in that it establishes a pattern for Larry's misguided interactions with others. Two white boys persuade him to shout a racist insult ('Monkey Lips') at a black girl, promising him as a reward membership in their group (without intending to keep their promise). Larry only makes a fool of himself, is severely bullied by his black classmates, ignored by his white 'friends', and reprimanded for his callous behavior by his teacher.

Larry's failures of judgement in interpersonal relations

Desperate for acceptance, Larry repeatedly falls for insincere offers and makes unwise decisions that have catastrophic consequences for him, for example:

- when he lends Silas a rifle belonging to his father,
- when he agrees to go on a date with Cindy Walker without stopping to question her true motives,

- when he starts his friendship with Wallace Stringfellow. After 25 years of isolation, Larry is so hungry for human companionship that he ignores Stringfellow's antisocial behavior and fails to report him to the police in spite of signs that the man has dangerous inclinations.

the symbolism of the rifle

In this chapter, the rifle that Larry borrows from his father's collection has an important symbolic significance:

- The rifle, belonging to his father, is a symbol of power and masculinity. Walking alone through the woods with the rifle, Larry is conforming – for once in his life – to the traditional southern image of the country boy.
- Furthermore, it gives him something that Silas doesn't have, but deeply desires. Silas is a complete novice with a gun, Larry something of an expert. This gives Larry a rare feeling of superiority and probably the vague hope that he can use this superiority to win Silas's friendship. That the rifle later leads to the rift between them, is one of the ironies of the plot.

Point to remember:

- Larry meets his half-brother Silas for the first time in March of 1979, when both are in eighth grade.
- Larry is an outsider at his school, not only because of his skin color.
- Larry and Silas begin hanging out together outside of school when Larry shows him how to use a rifle.

Chapter Four

Summary: After receiving Angie's call, Silas informs French of the shooting, then drives to the Otts' house, where he waits for French to arrive. The men search the house and barn for clues, but except for the blood stains, they find nothing suspicious. Silas makes plaster casts of car tracks and footprints in the mud outside the house. When Silas arrives home late that evening, he sees that he has a message on his answering machine. It is from Larry Ott, who called Monday morning to say that he had something important to tell him.

Commentary: The relationship between the (white) chief inspector and the (black) constable becomes more evident here than it was in Chapter Two. French is the one who makes the decisions and gives orders; Silas is the one who obeys. When Silas shows initiative by following up on a 'hunch' and is proven correct, French is not altogether pleased. Unlike Silas, French seems to be dominated by pre-formed opinions and attitudes. In the case of Larry Ott, he jumps to the conclusion that Larry has shot himself, never wondering why someone who wanted to die would shoot himself in the chest and not in the head, which would be far simpler and more effective. He collects fingerprints from all over the house, but apparently doesn't think to have Larry's right hand tested for traces of gunpowder. His blindness is symptomatic of a community that has regarded Larry for 25 years as a suspicious character and a potential danger, ever since Cindy Walker disappeared. Silas knows Larry better than anyone else in Chabot, in spite of their lack of contact – and Silas knows that Larry had nothing to do with Cindy's disappearance (we learn the reason why later in the novel). The fact that Larry urgently wanted to talk to Silas – in spite of the latter's refusal to have anything to do with him – suggests that someone (Larry's assailant) wanted to silence Larry before he could pass on incriminating information to the police.

Silas and CI French have differing views on Larry.

Chapter Five

Summary: Chapter Five begins on the first day of summer vacation after the eighth grade (for Larry and Silas). In retrospect, it describes the short-lived friendship between Silas and Larry, ending with the incident that marks the end of their friendship.

Since the two boys first met outside of school, they have spent much of their free time together in the woods, where Larry has shown Silas how to catch fish and entertains him with gruesome stories from Stephen King. In the course of their conversations Silas lets Larry know that he also has to keep their friendship hidden from his mother, as she has expressly forbidden him to associate with Larry.

Afraid that he might be losing Silas's interest, Larry leads him to the Walkers' house, hoping to find the teenage daughter Cindy sunbathing on the front porch. Larry has sometimes spied on her from the woods. This afternoon, Cindy's stepfather Cecil and Larry's father are sitting together on the porch, both drunk. When Cindy comes out wrapped in a bath towel and starts arguing with Cecil, the latter begins pulling the towel away from her, until Silas suddenly steps out of the woods and tells him to let go. Cindy goes back into the house, and Silas disappears before the white men can recover from their surprise.

Silas 'rescues' Cindy from her stepfather.

When Larry arrives at home, his father is waiting for him in a foul mood and demands to know where his rifle is. Larry doesn't say, but Carl guesses that he has given it to Silas. Carl demands that Larry bring the rifle back the following day. When Larry goes to the cabin the next morning, his father follows him. He deliberately provokes Silas, then says that he can keep the rifle if he beats Larry in a fight, threatening to whip them both if they refuse. Within seconds Silas has Larry pinned to the ground. When Silas refuses to let him go, Larry calls him 'nigger'. Silas allows him to stand up, then sends him to the ground again with a sharp blow to the head. When Larry comes to, he sees his father staggering in the grass as Silas runs away.

Carl Ott forces his sons to fight.

Commentary: The ill-fated friendship between Larry and his black half-brother Silas is shown in this chapter on two levels, the racial and the personal. The boys know that their friendship would not be condoned by their parents (or for that matter, by their peers). Larry seems to accept the overt racism of white society as given, but is surprised to hear from Silas that his mother feels the same way about relations between black and white. Their friendship can only thrive in the wilderness, where the rules of society have no validity.

no place for interracial friendship

In a symbolic sense, Carl Ott forces his sons to acknowledge the fundamental animosity between black and white by making the two boys fight. At the same time, he is fully aware that both of the boys are his sons. His cruel perversion of family bonds has an element of self-destruction, as if he were trying to punish fate for its injustice in giving him two sons he must be ashamed of. Larry senses that this episode has destroyed the relationship between him and Silas, that with the racist epithet 'nigger' he has pushed Silas back across the invisible line that separates black and white: '*Somewhere behind him he heard their voices and looked back to a world that would never be the same*' (p. 107, ll. 8 ff.).

Larry and Silas: a problematic friendship

On the personal level, we see that the friendship between the two boys is based on inequality and is ultimately too weak to bridge the gulf that separates them. Larry knows how to use a gun and fishing tackle; Silas doesn't, and is glad to profit from Larry. By lending Silas the rifle, Larry has given some of his power over his new friend. In other respects, the boys have diverging interests and attitudes:

- Larry is a bookworm; Silas is athletic, loves sports and the outdoors, but finds reading too difficult to be enjoyable.
- Larry finds the story about Cecil throwing fireworks at his stepdaughter amusing; Silas doesn't see anything funny about it and calls Cecil's behavior 'mean'.
- When Cecil molests his stepdaughter in front of Larry's father, it is Silas who bravely steps out into the open and tells him to leave the girl alone. Larry hides in the bushes, where he has often hidden in the past, secretly hoping to catch a glimpse of Cindy's bare skin, even though he privately fantasizes about Cindy seeking his help (p. 56, ll. 17 f.).

The growing rift between the two boys is emphasized at the end of the scene (p. 98, ll. 1–7), when Silas accuses Larry of spying on people and not helping Cindy when she needed it. In spite of his skin color, which in this case puts him at risk, Silas stands up for what he thinks is right, whereas Larry, lacking in self-esteem and perhaps taking a secret voyeuristic pleasure in Cindy's plight, lacks the strength of character to risk an open conflict with adults.

Points to remember:

- The friendship between Larry and Silas only lasts from February to June, when both boys are 14.
- The friendship between them is one-sided and is based mainly on Larry's desire for companionship.
- Carl Ott drives a wedge between them by forcing them to fight.

Chapter Six

Summary: On Wednesday morning, Silas goes first to Larry's garage, where he looks around briefly, then to Larry's house, where he finds a few scraps of evidence while looking around the grounds. Afterwards he examines the barn, feeds the chickens, then goes into the house, where he discovers a trapdoor leading to the attic. The attic houses mainly boxes of old documents and photographs, among them a photograph showing his mother with baby Larry.

Silas finds a photo linking his mother to the Otts.

There follows a flashback to his earlier life in Chicago with his mother and a man named Oliver, her mother's boyfriend. They lived a respectable life in a quiet, all-black neighborhood until Oliver got into serious trouble with the police. Alice put her house up for bail, i.e. she agreed that the state could claim ownership to her house if Oliver didn't appear in court, but Oliver, who knew that he had no chance of escaping a prison sentence, vanished before he came up for trial. Alice sold whatever she

Silas as a boy in Chicago

could and left in a hurry with Silas for her old home in Mississippi. On the way there Silas and his mother quarrel when she accepts help from a white man, they are robbed and lose most of their possessions. In the end, they reach Chabot and move into the cabin on the Otts' land.

Alice and her son leave Chicago for Mississippi.

Commentary: Chapter Six is the only chapter in which we observe Alice Jones as an active participant in the plot. She makes the impression of a strong-willed young woman who, however, knows the limits of her possibilities in a white- and male-dominated society. Silas observes that her behavior toward white people is not genuine (p. 130, ll. 18 f.); she knows how to ingratiate herself with them when she is dependent on them for help. Aware of her beauty, she prostitutes herself when necessary to gain favors from white men. Toward Silas she can be very strict; she reproaches herself with having spared him the experience of genuine hardship (p. 128, ll. 18 ff.).

interaction of Alice with white people

It is interesting to observe how the author presents a nuanced view of black and white characters in this chapter. The black characters in the chapter – except for Silas and his mother – are selfish, ruthless and pitiless:

black and white characters

- Oliver exploits Alice's love and leaves her all but penniless.
- The young thieves who steal their possessions have no empathy.

Where Alice and her son experience kindness and generosity, it comes from southern whites:

- Charles, the truck driver;
- the white woman at the bus station who brings Silas hot chocolate and a pair of shoes;
- the waitress in the diner in Fulsom who invents a story as an excuse to treat Alice to a free breakfast without injuring her pride.

The behavior of these white people contrasts markedly with the depraved behavior of Cecil and Carl in the previous chapter.

For Silas, the flight from Chicago is a disaster. He leaves a secure and comfortable life in the big city for one of bitter poverty in a rural region whose rules he does not understand. His first independent venture in Mississippi ends with him being robbed in a dark alleyway. Increasingly, his relationship to his mother becomes strained: on the one hand, he is repelled by her behavior toward white men, on the other hand he senses that he is an obstacle to her tenacious quest for survival.

Silas's new life: a turn for the worse

Points to remember:

- While searching the Otts' house for clues Silas discovers an old photograph showing that his mother once worked as a maid for the Ott family.
- There is an underlying tension between Silas and his mother Alice ever since she tore him away from his accustomed life and returned with him to her native Mississippi.

Chapter Seven

Summary: The seventh chapter relates in flashback the events that dramatically changed Larry's life. One day in 1982, when Larry is 16, Cindy Walker, the daughter of the Otts' nearest neighbors, unexpectedly asks Larry to take her to the drive-in cinema near Fulsom the following Friday. Larry makes plans for what he thinks will be the biggest event of his life, but when Cindy gets into the car on Friday evening, she tells him that she needs his help so that she can meet her boyfriend secretly. She drives with him to a remote spot, then gets out of the car, telling him to meet her at the turnoff to their road at 11 pm. Larry is crushed and mystified, but does what she

Larry's 'date' with Cindy (1982)

tells him to do, even going to the drive-in for a while and pretending that Cindy is with him. He arrives at their appointed meeting place a quarter of an hour early and waits an hour and a half before deciding that Cindy must have walked home without him. When he drives past the Walkers' house, Cecil Walker furiously accosts him, demanding to know where Cindy is. The police are called; the policeman tries to calm everyone down, saying that Cindy will probably turn up the next day.

When days pass with no sign of Cindy Walker, Larry is summoned to the police station for questioning. All attempts to locate Cindy lead to nothing. As her body is never found, the charges against Larry are dropped, but for the people of Chabot, Larry is the one responsible for the girl's disappearance. Larry stops going to school; his father loses customers and begins drinking heavily, his mother withdraws from local social life and shows increasing signs of memory loss. Larry joins the army and serves until he learns of his father's death in a car accident. He returns to Chabot and takes up his father's garage business.

the consequences of Cindy's disappearance for Larry

Commentary: In the first part of the chapter, the narrative perspective gives us access to Larry's thoughts and feelings as he prepares for his first date. For the awkward, unattractive Larry, it seems as if a dream has miraculously come true. Because we, the readers, do not share his blindness, we feel a sense of foreboding: something is wrong here. A pretty, popular girl like Cindy doesn't ruin her reputation by going out with a loser like Larry (or if she does, there must be something else behind it). The distance we feel toward Larry's feelings of elation is called **dramatic irony**. The author uses it here effectively to create the feeling that Larry's expectations are based on a completely false perception of the situation and that disaster is just around the corner.

the effect of the narrative perspective

Cindy's disappearance marks a turning point in Larry's life. Unable to explain what really happened, Larry puts up a weak defense, and, lacking a better explanation, public opinion is more than willing to believe that 'Scary Larry', the horror fan, is somehow responsible for the girl's disappearance. Larry needn't go to court, but the community pronounces him guilty anyway and makes him a pariah, an outsider no one wants anything to do with.

Larry is ostracized by the community.

The author gives mixed signals as to what was really behind Cindy's disappearance. In the car on the way to Fulsom, Cindy tells Larry that she wants to get away from her stepfather. From what we have seen of Cecil in Chapter 5, we can easily imagine that the man is secretly pursuing his stepdaughter behind his wife's back. The fact that Cecil calls her a '*little whore*' (p. 146, l. 13) points in the same direction: if Cindy is a 'whore', then she has no claim to protection from sexual abuse. On the other hand, when Larry returns shortly after midnight without Cindy, Cecil appears to be genuinely furious. If he had raped and murdered her, he would have to be play-acting in front of Larry, his wife and the police. Cindy also tells Larry that she is pregnant (but not from Cecil) and fears

What really happened to Cindy?

the consequences if it is discovered. Perhaps she wants to discuss the possibility of getting an (illegal) abortion with her boyfriend. The white boys Larry associates with at school contribute a further explanation: one of them says that Cindy *'likes niggers'* (p. 139, l. 4). Later we learn that Cindy and Silas were secretly going together at this time. Probably this has not altogether escaped the attention of her classmates. Cindy is doubtless afraid of the consequences if her stepfather found out that her boyfriend is black. Ultimately, Cindy's disappearance remains an unsolved mystery.

Points to remember:

- Larry sees Cindy Walker for the last time when he drops her off on a lonely road near Fulsom, where she wants to meet her boyfriend.
- There is no evidence that Larry had anything to do with Cindy's disappearance, but most people in Chabot believe that he raped and murdered her and somehow managed to hide her body. From this moment on, the fortunes of the Ott family decline dramatically. They are ostracized, and Larry is marked as a psychopathic murderer.

Chapter Eight

Summary: Chapter Eight continues the account of the events of Wednesday, the day after the shooting. Silas meets Angie at the local diner at lunch time. Here he tells her – evidently for the first time – about his past life: his friendship with Larry Ott and how it ended, the time when Larry was asked to play the monster at a Halloween event and then was snubbed by his classmates. Angie asks him about Cindy Walker, but Silas avoids mentioning his own connection with the white girl. After lunch Silas goes to the hospital and asks about Larry's condi-

Silas tells Angie about his relationship to Larry.

tion. He is told that Larry is stable but still unconscious. Silas asks the receptionist if Larry has had any visitors and gives him his telephone number, asking to be informed if anyone does come to visit. Then he goes to the River Acres Nursing Home to tell Mrs. Ott what has happened, but the mother is so disoriented that Silas gives up, asking the nurse to inform him when her mental condition improves.

Silas stops Stringfellow and later discovers a fresh grave.

On the way to the old hunting cabin where he once lived, Silas stops Wallace Stringfellow for driving illegally with a four-wheeler on private property. Silas lets him go with a warning, then drives on to the cabin. The house is locked and overgrown with vegetation, but Silas finds a broken window pane on one side and shines his flashlight into the room, where he discovers a freshly dug grave in the dirt floor.

Commentary: On the one level, Silas is investigating the Larry Ott case, visiting Larry's workshop and house, the hospital where he is being treated, attempting to inform his mother. Beneath the surface, he is being confronted with his own past, a past he has repressed from memory the past twenty-five years. The photograph he finds at the Otts' house leads him back to his mother and the diner where she worked for twenty years. His feelings of guilt begin to surface:

Silas's feelings of guilt

- his guilt toward his mother, for neglecting her and refusing to honor her sacrifice.
- his guilt toward Larry, for betraying their friendship and ignoring him when he tried to re-establish contact.
- his guilt regarding Cindy Walker, a sensitive point he is not able to deal with yet.

The incident in which Larry is asked to play the 'monster' at a Halloween event during his junior year at high school is of great symbolic significance for the novel.

Once again, Larry dreams in vain of belonging, of being rewarded for compliance with acceptance by the others. But as it turns out, Larry is accepted only in the monster role; when he takes his mask off and becomes Larry Ott again, he is demonstratively ignored by his classmates – in particular by Silas, who describes Larry's departure in great detail (p. 165, l. 26–p. 166, l. 14), as if to call the reader's attention to his own sin of omission. This behavior on the part of the other students mirrors the community's treatment of Larry Ott in later years: he lives on in their memory as 'Scary Larry', the psychopath, whereas Larry Ott the human being has long since faded from their minds.

Larry's Halloween performance: symbolism

In this chapter we also find the first confirmation that Silas knows who his father is (p. 175, l. 17 ff.). It is important to note that Silas's recollection of the only time he ever visited the Otts' house is closely linked with his longing for a father. Unlike Larry, Silas finds mowing the lawn great fun and insists on mowing the whole yard on his own. When Carl Ott suddenly returns, Silas runs off into the woods, but hears how Carl praises his son for his good work. Ironically, the black boy Silas is the kind of son Carl would have been proud of, whereas for his white son he feels only contempt (p. 103, ll. 24 ff.).

Silas misses having a father.

Points to remember:

- Silas is aware that he and Larry Ott have the same father.
- Silas feels guilty about his mother, Larry and Cindy Walker.

Chapter Nine

Summary: This chapter relates the story of the relationship between Larry Ott and Wallace Stringfellow. It begins around 1996, when Larry is 31. Larry notices that someone has been secretly entering his barn and disturbing or even stealing things. One day he hides in the barn, waiting for the intruder, then jumps out wearing his zombie mask. A blond boy runs away and the trouble stops. Ten years later, Wallace Stringfellow comes to the Otts' house pretending to be working for a firm that installs satellite dishes. Larry shows interest, but Stringfellow doesn't return as he promised. Two months later, he comes back again, this time on a four-wheeler, and pretends that he was fired by his firm. Later he admits that he told Larry a lie and tries to win Larry's trust. Larry recognizes him as the boy who used to snoop around his barn. Larry feels uncomfortable in his presence, as Stringfellow usually gets drunk and smokes marijuana on his premises, but it is the first real company he has had in years, and so he tolerates Stringfellow's alcohol and drug consumption. When Larry tells him that teenagers have come in the night and damaged his truck, he gives him a small pistol as a Christmas present. Stringfellow asks Larry about the murder of Cindy Walker, assuring him that he would never betray his friend, and doesn't seem to accept Larry's claim that he is innocent. On another occasion, he admits that he has also been in the cabin that was once used by Silas and his mother, and that he has fantasies about Larry holding him there as a prisoner. He goes on to fantasize about raping a girl, talking himself into sexual arousal. Larry, repelled by his behavior, tells him to go home. Stringfellow flies into a rage and smashes the headlights and windshield of Larry's truck before driving off. His regular

Larry's relationship with Stringfellow

String-fellow's fantasies

visits end. Larry tries to reach him by telephone, but soon gives up.

the reader as detective

Commentary: Author Tom Franklin follows a time-honored tradition by allowing the reader to slip into the role of the detective, collecting information, sorting the relevant from the irrelevant, and drawing plausible conclusions. We know from Chapter One that Larry was shot by someone wearing Larry's zombie mask. We also know that Larry had a small pistol in his hand when he was found. Wallace Stringfellow also knew that Larry had the mask and the pistol. Moreover, he had been snooping around the area for years and knew where he could gain entrance to locked buildings. He has also discovered the cabin in the woods, where, as we now know, a fresh grave has been dug. When we hear that Stringfellow has fantasies about imprisonment and rape, it becomes clear that he is the most likely culprit, both for the death of Tina Rutherford and for the attack on Larry Ott.

As the narrative perspective (→Narrative Structure, p. 62) jumps back and forth between Larry (who is presently unable to give any information to the police) and Silas, the reader is better informed than any of the individual figures of the plot. This creates a kind of dramatic irony that is typical of detective stories: while the characters involved grope in the dark, we the readers watch the web of detection draw closer and closer.

Stringfellow: a false friend

Stringfellow is the last in a series of 'false friends' who abuse Larry for their own purposes. Himself a loner, Stringfellow senses that Larry is desperate for companionship and will not send him away, no matter how he behaves. With the Christmas present of the pistol, he attempts to court Larry's favor. Tormented by his own evil inclinations, Stringfellow believes that in Larry he has found a kindred spirit. He is convinced (like everyone else) that Larry raped and murdered Cindy Walker and eagerly tries to get Larry to share the details with him.

When Larry refuses to admit his guilt, Stringfellow ends their relationship in a rampage, evidently feeling that all his efforts have been for nothing and that his so-called 'friend' doesn't trust him. There is a bitter irony in the fact that Larry owes his only social contact, not to his gentle, self-effacing character, but to his (erroneous) public image as a perverse killer, and that he loses this contact by refusing to conform to expectations, instead insisting on his personal integrity.

Chapter Ten

Summary: Chapter Ten begins on Monday of the week following the attack on Larry Ott. Silas looks back on the events following the discovery of Tina Rutherford's body and tells Angie about his relationship with Cindy Walker in 1982.

Tina's body is found: the aftermath.

Tina's corpse was found buried in the grave Silas had discovered in the cabin where he had once lived. With his third discovery of a victim in two days, Silas has become a local celebrity. It is generally assumed that Larry Ott is Tina's murderer, and so a police guard has been stationed at his door 24 hours a day. Silas asks to be given the night shift. On one occasion, the receptionist tells him that a '*stringy-looking*' young white man had been there to ask about Larry's condition. During his own shift, Silas wakes up to see a '*stringy-looking*' figure standing in the dark watching him. The man runs off when he sees that Silas is awake.

On Monday afternoon, Silas drives to the nursing home, having been told by a staff member that Larry's mother was having a 'good day'. He shows her the photograph of his mother holding Larry, and Mrs. Ott remembers their black maid who had to leave when she became pregnant. When Silas tries to find out who the father was, however, her memory fails her.

flashback: Silas's relationship with Cindy

On Monday evening, Silas meets Angie for dinner and tells her the story of his involvement with Cindy Walker. Silas noticed that Cindy regularly came to baseball games whenever he was playing. One day she waited for him, and they walked home together. They immediately felt attracted to each other and soon began meeting regularly, always in secret. Somehow Silas's mother found out that he was seeing a white girl and urged him to stop.

Cindy also came under pressure: Cecil accused her of having promiscuous sex and forbade her to leave the house except for school. On the other hand, Cindy told Silas that Cecil sexually molested her. She used Larry as an excuse to get out of the house and meet Silas. Cindy wanted him to run away with her, but Silas refused, and they quarreled. Finally, he drove her back to her turnoff, and Cindy ran down the road toward her house and disappeared. Silas left for Oxford High School two months later, thinking that Cindy had run off and would turn up sooner or later. His busy life in high school and later at college let him forget about the events back in Chabot.

The chapter ends early Tuesday, when Silas is at the Otts' house, feeding the chickens. He gets a phone call from the receptionist at the hospital, who tells him that Larry Ott has regained consciousness.

Commentary: Silas supplies one of the last missing pieces in the Cindy Walker case. He was the mysterious boyfriend she wanted to meet secretly the evening she disappeared. Even in 1982, a mixed-race couple was evidently taboo in the part of the country where the two teenagers lived.

Cindy's fate is never conclusively revealed in the novel. Silas supposes that Cecil must have killed her (p. 232, ll. 7 f.). As Cindy was last seen running down the road to her house and Cecil was at home alone when she arrived, it is not impossible that he murdered her and hid her body before his wife came home from work. There is, however, no proof, and a motive is missing. We know that Cecil has molested his stepdaughter, and it is not difficult to imagine him abusing her while drunk. On the other hand, Cindy herself says that her mother always stood by her husband, that Cecil had actually complained to her about Cindy provoking him sexually, and that her mother was evidently inclined to believe him, not her daughter (p. 229). His only motive for murdering Cindy and disposing of her body would be to hide the traces of his misdeed. But if he had no cause to fear his wife's reaction, why risk murder? Moreover, it would mean that Cecil was play-acting when he grabbed Larry by the collar and angrily demanded to know what he had done with his stepdaughter (cf. Commentary, Chapter Seven). This is probably more than Cecil is capable of.

Was Cindy murdered by her stepfather?

Chapter Eleven

Summary: Larry opens his eyes and begins to appraise his situation. As he has been pumped full of drugs to combat the pain, he is still very groggy and has difficulty

Larry regains conscious-ness.

separating dream and reality. When the staff see that Larry is conscious, they inform French, who appears with Sheriff Lolly to interrogate him. When Larry learns from them that Tina Rutherford has been found raped and murdered, he goes into convulsions, and the doctor ends the questioning.

When he regains consciousness, French and Lolly resume the interrogation. French uses highly suggestive language to persuade Larry to confess to murdering Cindy Walker and the Rutherford girl. Larry's brief answers reveal little. His only request – to be allowed to talk to Silas – is denied.

French wants Larry to confess.

Chapter Twelve

Summary: Chapter Twelve takes up where the previous chapter ends, in the middle of the interrogation. Silas arrives at the hospital, afraid that Larry will give in to pressure and confess, and bursts into Larry's room. He shocks the two white police officers by telling them that he was the one Cindy wanted to meet the night she disappeared and that Larry had told the truth all along – he had nothing to do with whatever happened to Cindy after he dropped her off.

Silas admits that he was Cindy's boyfriend.

The police officers end the interrogation and take Silas to the Sheriff's Department, where Silas gives an account of the events of 1982 from his point of view. French makes clear to him that even though Larry had nothing to do with Cindy's disappearance, he is still the prime suspect in the Rutherford case, as few people knew of the existence of the abandoned hunting cabin on the Otts' land.

Silas tells French about his relationship to Cindy.

Silas goes back to the hospital and tries to persuade Larry to reveal what he wanted to tell him when he phoned the day before he was shot. Larry is upset that Silas let him bear the blame for Cindy's death for 25 years

Larry refuses to talk to Silas.

in spite of knowing that he was innocent. Silas is convinced that Larry knows who shot him, but Larry refuses to give him the information he wants. That evening, Silas unexpectedly receives a new clue when Irina, one of the young women who called the police because of the snake in their mailbox, appears at the bar where he is sitting alone and tells him about a housemate of hers named Evelyn, who for a time went out with a 'weird' man named Wallace Stringfellow. One night she went home with him and saw that he had a snake collection. When she resisted his advances, he got violent. Evelyn managed to grab the pistol she kept in her handbag and escaped unharmed. Irina thinks this could be the same person who put the snake in their mailbox. Silas remembers that he once stopped Stringfellow on a private road, that he had a pillowcase with him, and that Larry had once told him that pillowcases were good for transporting snakes. Silas drives Irina home, although they are both very drunk. Irina wants him to stay, but Silas decides it would be wiser to leave.

Irina tells Silas about Stringfellow's violent behavior.

Commentary: In this chapter Larry and Silas communicate again for the first time in 25 years (with the exception of a very brief phone call two years before the story begins). The past weighs heavily on both of them:

- Larry feels guilty for calling his only friend a 'nigger'.
- Silas feels guilty a) for cutting Larry out of his life, b) for refusing to come out of hiding when Larry was accused of murder, c) for rejecting Larry's attempts at re-establishing contact.

Silas and Larry: a difficult relationship

In the present situation, Silas is mainly interested in getting Larry to give him whatever information he has on his assailant; Larry is still shocked by the revelation that Silas was the mysterious boyfriend Cindy wanted to see that fateful night.

It is worth noting that Larry twice asks Silas if they were friends back then, in 1979. The first time (p. 247,

l. 17), Silas confirms their friendship. Before the police leave, Larry again asks Silas if they were once friends (p. 250, ll. 8 f.). This time Silas hesitates. We see in italics what is going through his head: *'Tell the fucking truth'* (l. 10). We can infer from this that Silas was lying when he told Larry that they had once been friends, and his answer this time is different: *'You were, Larry [...]. I don't know what I was.'* For Larry, who has been a loner most of his life, the matter is relatively simple; for Silas, the relationship with Larry was a secret life he lived apart from his 'real' life at home and at school (and in this regard analogous to his clandestine relationship with Cindy Walker).

Points to remember:

- When Larry awakens from his coma, he learns that Silas was Cindy Walker's mysterious boyfriend.
- From this moment on, Larry feels betrayed by Silas and refuses to cooperate with him.

Chapter Thirteen

Summary: Larry is lying alone in his hospital room watching television and thinking about his new situation. Zapping through the sixty-something channels on cable TV, Larry begins to realize how much the world has changed in the past 25 years. Larry recalls something important and asks the police officer stationed outside his room if he can speak to French, who, however, has left town. Larry remembers that Wallace Stringfellow appeared one night in front of his house and indirectly confessed to having 'done' something. Larry is certain that Wallace was his assailant and probably the murderer of Tina Rutherford.

Commentary: Lying awake in his hospital bed, Larry begins to critically examine his behavior and his understanding of the word *'friend'* (p. 264, ll. 18–26). Until now, Larry has understood friendship to mean accommodation, doing what the other person expects from you. Now he realizes that he has been exploited and abandoned by those he believed were his friends: *'maybe he'd been shoved away from everybody for so long all he was was a sponge for the wrongs other people did'* (p. 264, ll. 22 ff.). Larry resolves to live his life differently, to make himself independent of what others think of him and to forge his own identity: *'Maybe, after all this time, he'd started to believe their version of him. But no more'* (p. 264, ll. 24 ff.).

Larry thinks about the meaning of friendship.

Chapter Fourteen

Summary: The following morning Silas wakes up at home with a splitting headache, goes to The Hub for breakfast, then to the town hall, where he learns that French is out of town for the day. He decides to look around Larry's house one more time and discovers fresh tire marks from a four-wheeler, the same tread marks he found there after the attack, as well as an empty beer can.

He remembers Wallace Stringfellow and decides to look into the matter with the snakes.

Silas drives over to the area where Stringfellow lives, finds a fierce-looking dog tied up in the front yard and a four-wheeler parked near the house. Stringfellow comes out and is disinclined to

Silas goes to question Stringfellow.

talk to him, but Silas insists on going into the house. There he sees that Stringfellow has a large collection of snakes in aquariums. Stringfellow is nervous and tries to get rid of his unwelcome guest, but Silas looks around the room at a leisurely pace. When he discovers the zombie mask that belonged to Larry, Stringfellow panics and steps outside, saying he wants to quiet the dog down. Instead he sets him loose. The dog attacks Silas, mangling his left arm. Stringfellow has a gun and fires at him, hitting the dog instead. Silas, who has crawled under the house for protection, finally manages to grab his pistol and kill the dog. Then he shoots at the fleeing Stringfellow, wounding him in the leg. Bleeding heavily from his wounds, Silas crawls back into the house and collapses.

Chapter Fifteen

Summary: Chapter Fifteen relates the incidents of the same day as Chapter Fourteen, but from Larry's point of view. Larry reminds the deputy sitting outside his room that he wants to talk to Chief French. When the afternoon comes and French still hasn't come to the hospital, Larry asks the deputy again and learns about the gunfight at Stringfellow's house. Larry says he has important information on Stringfellow, and the deputy gets French on the radio. Larry tells him why he is sure that Stringfellow is the man who shot him as well as the murderer of Tina Rutherford.

Larry tells French about Stringfellow.

That evening French comes to the hospital to talk to Larry. He tells him that Silas is in recovery and that Stringfellow is dead. Then he asks Larry questions about his relationship to Stringfellow. Larry begins to feel guilty, thinking that he could have prevented a tragedy if he had acted differently. Then the door to his room is pushed open and Silas is wheeled in.

Larry's guilty feelings

Chapter Sixteen

Summary: Before dawn the next morning, Silas wakes up while Larry is watching the news on TV. The newscaster reports on the latest developments in the Rutherford case. Tina Rutherford's wallet was discovered in Stringfellow's house, pointing to Stringfellow as the murderer. When the news ends, Silas talks to Larry about their past, asking him if Larry knew all along that they are half-brothers. Larry first denies it, then admits that he suspected as much. After a while Larry calls the nurse and asks if it would be possible for him to have a separate room.

Silas and Larry talk.

Chapter Seventeen

Summary: Later that day Angie comes to visit Silas. Then she goes over to Larry's bed and talks to him, saying that he is welcome to come to the black Baptist church if he wants. Larry thanks her for saving his life after the shooting.

The next day, the town clerk, the mayor and later CI French come to visit. French informs the two patients that evidence has been found linking Stringfellow to the shooting of Larry Ott as well as to the murder of Morton Morrisette. French removes the leather restraints on Larry's wrists. Shortly after he leaves, Silas is discharged from hospital. Larry is offered a different room, but refuses.

Larry is freed.

Chapter Eighteen

Summary: After Silas has met with a police reporter to tell his story, Angie drives him to the town hall, where he learns that Mr. Rutherford has offered to finance a part-time traffic warden to give Silas more time for police work, and that the town is seeking to replace his Jeep with a newer model. Then Silas goes with Angie to her place, where she plans to look after him for a few days while he recovers.

The day after, Silas goes to Larry Ott's house to collect the mail and feed the chickens, then he brings Larry his mail and visits Mrs. Ott at the nursing home. When he is feeling better, he goes with Angie to Larry's house to clean up. While Angie scrubs the floor to remove the blood stains, Silas cleans out the gun cabinet and puts the rifle he got from Larry when they were boys back in its place.

Silas returns the rifle to its proper place.

Commentary: Silas is driven by the feeling that he has something to 'make good for' in his life, i.e. he has failed in several ways in the past and now wants to make up for it. By putting the rifle back in its proper place, Silas is symbolically restoring order to their world. Once a symbol of the rivalry between the two half-brothers, the rifle becomes the symbol of a new beginning. (→Language and Imagery, p. 72)

Chapter Nineteen

Summary: During the days after Silas's release from hospital, he starts bringing Larry clothes and personal belongings from home, preparing him for his return to normal life. On the fifth day, Larry's physician tells him that he is satisfied with Larry's condition and urges him to get out of bed and walk around. Larry gets up and goes down to the lobby, looking out at the waiting journalists standing in the parking lot.

That night, Larry gets up, dresses, and leaves the hospital. He has the wish to go home, or at least to his workshop, but soon realizes that he is still too weak to walk

Larry leaves the hospital.

that far on his own. The night receptionist at the hospital observed Larry's departure and phones Silas, who climbs into his Jeep and drives down the highway until he finds Larry and takes him to his house. On the way there they talk about the old Jeep Silas still drives; Larry wants to repair it. Silas gives him his wallet, keys and cell phone, and Larry goes into his house, where Silas and Angie have left fresh flowers and food. Larry looks around the house and discovers the rifle that he lent Silas 27 years earlier.

Silas finds Larry and drives him home.

Commentary: The final chapters of the novel are much shorter than the earlier ones. They have the function of what is called **denouement**, meaning that the various 'open ends' of the story are brought to some kind of conclusion:

- Tina's murderer and Larry Ott's assailant is found.
- Stringfellow is linked to the murder of Morton Morrisette.
- Cindy Walker's disappearance is officially attributed to Cecil Walker.
- Larry Ott is exonerated from all suspicions and returns to 'normal' life.
- Silas admits the role he played in Cindy Walker's disappearance.
- Silas and Larry admit their true identity and begin rebuilding their relationship as friends and half-brothers.

denouement: tying up the loose ends

The Characters

Main characters

Larry Ott

Larry and his relationship with his parents

Larry is the victim of heredity and his ambivalent upbringing. His parents are ill-matched (see below) and seldom see eye-to-eye on anything. Physically, he takes after his mother – a great misfortune in his case, as his father is tall, handsome and athletic, whereas Larry resembles the effeminate brothers on his mother's side of the family tree (p. 49, ll. 21 ff.; p. 50, ll. 23 ff.). As a boy, he was sickly and frail (asthma, allergies, stuttering, poor eyesight). As his mother was constantly worried about his health, she became overprotective, going to his bedside every night (p. 100, l. 20) and praying to God to help her ailing, unhappy son. Larry grows up emotionally dependent on his mother, who always takes his side in quarrels with her husband (p. 98, l. 16–p. 100, l. 13). Even when, as a teenager, he wants to go out on his first date, he is too timid to ask his father if he can borrow his mother's car; his mother has to ask for him (p. 133, ll. 26–32). Larry is afraid of his father, who despises him and lets him feel it (p. 49, l. 18); for Carl Ott, his son is a disappointment and a source of embarrassment:

'In the olden days you'd a been dead a long time ago. Some Indian cutting your throat or some gook with a grenade. You got it easy. Momma's boy reading the livelong day. Watch your cartoons, play with your dolls, read your funny books. But you can't unscrew a god dang bolt to save your life, can't charge a dad blame battery. And here when it comes to knuckles, you can't even get your own daddy's gun back from the boy that stole it.' (p. 103, ll. 25–31)

Larry's low self-esteem

Larry's father undermines his son's self-esteem by asserting that he is mechanically inept and refusing to take him to the garage with him. As we see later in the novel, Larry learns auto mechanics while in the army, and his idea of a moveable pen for his chickens is both ingenious and ecologically progressive. But the feeling that he is useless leaves him permanently morose and stand-offish, an obvious victim for bullies in his youth and a misanthropic recluse in his later years.

Larry's reading habits

Larry escapes through books from the world he is so ill-equipped for. His favorite author is evidently Stephen King. His love of literature – something he shares with no one else of his peer group – makes him even more of an outsider and a recluse. His taste for horror suggests that there is something sadistic in Larry's character, that he perhaps indulges in revenge fantasies; he mentions, for example, two stories in which machines rebel and do horrible things to people. However, it seems that Larry enjoys horror only on the vicarious level; when Wallace Stringfellow begins fantasizing about rape and torture, Larry is disgusted and turns his back on him (p. 203, ll. 1 ff.).

Larry as a teenager: character traits

As a teenager Larry is awkward, befuddled and naïve. When an attractive girl asks him to go out with her, he doesn't think to question her motives. He patiently allows his school chums and his mother to bombard him with superfluous advice; he allows Cecil to manhandle him and Cindy to boss him around. When Cindy tells him that they are not going on a date at all, instead of getting angry Larry merely whines, '*Can't we just go to the movie?*' (p. 149, ll. 27 f.), then does what she wants him to do. Cindy's mysterious disappearance and the ensuing investigations leave him dumbfounded and helpless. Although he knows that he is innocent, he is too unsure of himself and too inarticulate to present his case convincingly. As a result, nobody believes him, and he is marked for life. Larry leaves Chabot and finds temporary refuge in the army, but never really 'belongs'. After his father's death he returns to Chabot to look after his 'momma' and goes into a kind of social hibernation that lasts 25 years, ostracized and vilified by the community. His isolation is only temporarily relieved through the visits of Wallace Stringfellow, a *'strange lonely kid'* (p. 264, l. 29) like Larry once was, who rekindles in him the need for human companionship.

Larry's brief friendship with Silas

The only bright spot in Larry's youth is his short-lived friendship with Silas. From the very start their relationship is asymmetric: Larry knows more and has more than Silas, but Larry, a friendless loner, is far more dependent on Silas than Silas is on him. There is an undercurrent of rivalry and jealousy in their relationship from the beginning. Silas finds it unfair that Larry's family should own so much while he and his mother own nothing (p. 174, l. 29–p. 175, l. 3). Larry generously shares what he has with Silas, but at the same time has a feeling of 'buying' the poorer boy's friendship (p. 91, ll. 4–9). Too desperate for companionship and too fearful of losing it, Larry doesn't know how to stand up to Silas over the rifle he lent him, for example. In a sense Larry is also jealous of Silas. He knows in his heart that Silas is the kind of son Carl would have wanted (p. 285, l. 31). When his father forces them to fight, effectively ending their friendship, Larry falls back on his only remaining shred of superiority – his race – by calling his friend a *'nigger'* (p. 106, l. 23).

Larry as an adult: character traits

As an adult, Larry is tolerant and self-effacing; although he is occasionally harassed by youth from the town, he ignores them and refuses to be provoked by them, patiently repairing the damage they do to his mailbox and his truck. He never reproaches Wallace with his erratic and devious behavior; even when Wallace flies into a drunken rage, threatening to denounce him and doing damage to his truck, Larry merely excuses himself and goes into the house (p. 204). Larry also has a keen conscience (in spite of the injustice he has experienced in his lifetime). When he hears what has happened to Tina Rutherford, Silas and Stringfellow, he is genuinely upset and reproaches himself for not having taken action earlier to warn the police (p. 281, ll. 5–14).

Points to remember:

- Larry is hampered in his development by an overprotective mother and an aggressive father who rejects him.
- Larry escapes through reading into a fantasy world, heightening his isolation.
- The only relief to his loneliness comes from the brief, one-sided friendship between Larry and Silas.
- Larry is too desperate for companionship and too lacking in self-esteem to deal appropriately and effectively with others (Silas, his father, Cindy, the police, Stringfellow).

Larry: key passages

- p. 49, ll. 18–24
  His weaknesses as a child are described.
- pp. 60–63
  His ostracization at school sets a pattern for his life.
- p. 103, ll. 19–31
  His father expresses his disappointment in him.
- p. 106, l. 23
  Larry ends his friendship with Silas by insulting him.
- p. 281, ll. 5–14
  Larry questions his own behavior and his inability to talk to Silas about his fears.

Silas Jones

Like Larry, Silas is in some ways a victim of circumstances: disowned by his father, raised by a single mother who cannot tell him the truth about his origins, Silas lacks the encouragement of a male role model. As he grows up, he feels this loss more keenly: 'Good work, boy. *Silas remembered it. He had felt, at that moment, most acutely in his life, the absence of a father*' (p. 174, ll. 27 ff.). He is strongly attached to his mother (p. 230, l. 10), upon whom he is completely dependent. At the same time, he feels that he is sometimes in the way. At a very early age he understands that his mother has to prostitute herself to get favors from white men (p. 124, ll. 10–14). He simply accepts this, just as he unquestioningly accepts his mother's authority. When she comes between him and his girlfriend Cindy, he decides in his mother's favor, ending the affair by refusing to run off with the white girl. Later, after moving to Oxford, he subconsciously rebels against his mother by ignoring her and the sacrifices she has made for him:

lack of a father figure

"His mother had had to work two jobs plus clean houses to pay for the trailer home she'd bought in Fulsom. Back then he'd told himself she just wanted him out of the way. That was why she'd sent him off. Lying to himself even as he opened the letters she mailed him in Oxford, unfolding the limp five- and ten-dollar bills she sent each week so he could go to his classes and play baseball without having to get a job. He knew now she'd loved him despite his never writing her back, despite the trouble and fear he caused her, despite the thing missing out of him. He'd returned her love by rarely coming home, and when he did she'd doted over him, as if every meal was his last, or hers, straightened his paper napkin and lain another chicken leg on his plate and filled his milk glass or his iced tea so much he could barely stand it. He'd refused to see the truth, that she was starving from loneliness. In fact, he could barely look at her. All he could do was eat quickly and squirm away and go out into the night (driving her car) and find M & M and his other high

school friends while she sat waiting for him to come home." (p. 177, l. 22–p. 178, l. 7).

Alice Jones blames herself for having raised Silas the wrong way, sparing him contact with real hardship:

"What's missing out of you, Silas?" She looked hard.

"You ain't seen it that bad. I know. I know cause I have seen it that bad. But you. Up till now you had it easier than I ever did. But now I see what kind of man it's made you, I don't know if maybe I didn't do you a disservice." (p. 128, ll. 15 ff.)

Ironically, her self-analysis closely parallels Carl Ott's criticism of Larry's upbringing (p. 103, ll. 25–31). Both half-brothers are in some ways 'momma's boys' who have never experienced the influence of a loving but strict father who teaches them what it means to be a man.

Silas accepts his mother's interpretation of his character as being in some sense deficient (*'What's missing out of you, Silas?'*). His answer is: *'courage'* (p. 234, ll. 13 f.). Silas bases his self-criticism on his failure to come out of hiding and admit the role he played in Cindy's disappearance (even though it would have cleared Larry's name). Even 25 years later, he finds it difficult to confess his complicity to his girlfriend Angie and his superior, CI French.

how Silas sees himself

The text of the novel tells a somewhat different story, suggesting that what Silas lacks is not so much courage as empathy. As a young boy, he doesn't understand his mother's feelings and motives:

Courage or empathy – which is missing?

Silas thinking how Mrs. Ott had driven away and Silas had put on his coat and zipped it to his neck and buried his hands in the pockets, which were lined with fur. But his mother had continued to stand in the freezing air, holding the coat she'd been given, looking at it. "Ain't you gone put it on, Momma?" he'd asked as they started to walk, her carrying the long gray coat as if someone had handed her a dead child. At some point Alice slipped one arm and then the other into the coat's sleeves, she buttoned its buttons, starting at the top. Silas had followed her, still not seeing what an emblem of defeat, shame, loss, hopelessness, the coat was. With such gaps in his understanding, he saw very clearly how the boy he'd been had grown to be the man he was. (p. 285, l. 32–286, l. 8)

Neither was he capable of realizing the effects of his actions (or inaction) on the lives of others:

"Things ain't so clear when they're happening, Angie. You're eighteen and playing ball and everything's going your way. Then all of a sudden twenty-five years've passed and the person you look back and see's a whole nother person. You don't even recognize who you used to be. Wasn't till I come back down here that I saw the mess I'd made." (p. 232, ll. 1 ff.)

Silas's strong points

In other situations, Silas displays both physical courage and the courage of his convictions. As a young boy, he walks up to two drunk white racists who are molesting a girl and fearlessly tells them off. As a police officer, he deals with rattlesnakes, attack dogs and armed killers with cool-headed professionalism.

Silas's weak points

Looking back on his past, Silas accuses himself of avoiding responsibility, of choosing the path of least resistance: *'Letting himself off the hook had been his way of life'* (p. 268, ll. 17 f.). In point of fact, the high hopes he had when he left Chabot all fizzle out. His career as a potential professional baseball player came to an abrupt end when he broke his elbow (p. 282, ll. 13 f.) at college. After that, he attends police academy, then joins the university police (instead of the city police force) until, years later, he goes back to the small rural backwater he once fled from. Although already 41, he talks about his 'girl' and his former 'girlfriends', as if he were still a teenager. In Marla (at The Hub) he has found a kind of ersatz mother who feeds him and comforts him when he is down. There is a hint in the novel that Silas suffered from a form of dyslexia when he was younger (p. 260, ll. 15–20). As his problem evidently remained undiagnosed, presumably his reading and spelling difficulties held him back during high school and college, lowering his self-esteem and thus his ambition. But ultimately it is the lack of a father's encouragement and example that undermines Silas's character. As a grown man, he is still living like a boy, self-centered and dependent, and shuns the idea of taking on responsibility for a family of his own (p. 37, ll. 22–25).

Points to remember:

- Like Larry, Silas grows up closely attached to his mother, on whom he is dependent.
- Silas thinks of himself as lacking in courage, but his lack of empathy is even more evident.
- Due to his sports injury, his lack of self-esteem and (possibly) dyslexia, Silas sets low goals for himself in life, ultimately returning to the hamlet he once fled.
- As an adult in his early forties, Silas still lives in some ways the lifestyle of a teenager.

Silas: key passages

- p. 177, l. 22–178, l. 7
  Silas ignores all the hard work that his mother has done for him.
- p. 231, l. 16–p. 232, l. 6
  Silas confesses that he forgot about Cindy and Larry (and his responsibility to them) when he left town.
- p. 234, ll. 13–14
  Silas admits he has no courage in facing uncomfortable facts.
- p. 268, ll. 17–18
  Silas says that letting himself off the hook had always been his way of coping with life.
- p. 295, ll. 11–25
  Silas tries to make up for his past mistakes by returning Larry's gun.

Larry and Silas in comparison

At one point in the story, Larry appears to think of Silas and himself as 'dopplegängers' (p. 55, ll. 16 f.), although in the dialogue at the dinner table it had been Larry and his Uncle Colin who were called dopplegängers by the uncle. While Larry and his half-brother bear little physical resemblance to each other, in other respects there are a number of parallels between them. Both of them suffer from being rejected by their father. Both are pampered by dominant, overprotective mothers. As a result, both of them suffer from low self-esteem, a problem that follows them into adulthood.

Larry and Silas: parallels

In other respects, their lives diverge in opposite directions. Larry stays in Chabot, living *'like a curator'* (p. 7, l. 8) in his parents' house, spending his lonely days at his father's garage, going through the motions as if his life were trapped in a never-ending past. Silas flees, looking for a better life in the big city, but returns 23 years later to Chabot, where he is confronted with his own past and finds his identity: *'I felt like I belonged here. It's part of why I came back, after all that time'* (p. 164, ll. 1 f.). While Larry, who has never left Chabot except for a brief stint in the army, is excluded from the community he belongs to, Silas is (outwardly) well integrated. Yet both men are linked by the secret Silas has kept to himself for 25 years. Larry suffers outwardly from the consequences of his half-brother's silence, whereas Silas suffers inwardly from his feelings of guilt and failure. In a certain sense, both men wear masks. Larry wears the 'monster mask' the community has forced on him; after 25 years, he begins to wonder if he hasn't become the monster others see in him (p. 264, ll. 24 f.). Silas – still referred to in Chabot by his schoolboy identity, '32' – hides the truth of his life behind a cool, self-confident façade. Both men must shed their masks and show their true faces, including the familial bond that links them – for both a painful process.

Larry and Silas: differences

Points to remember:

- Silas and Larry have a similarity in their relationships to their parents.
- While Larry is forced to suffer outwardly through ostracism, Silas suffers inwardly from his feelings of guilt and cowardice.
- Both men must learn to face the truth and take on responsibility for their lives.

Minor characters

Carl and Ina Ott

Larry's parents: a mismatch

Larry's parents give the impression that their marriage only works because they avoid each other as much as possible and in other cases adhere to strict rules. They are fundamentally ill-suited to each other and differ radically in their interests and attitudes. The inherent ambivalence in their notions of how to raise their son has serious consequences for Larry.

Carl Ott: character traits

Carl is depicted as a gifted mechanic and a popular storyteller whose workshop is a kind of informal meeting place for white men of his age group. Working with his hands, getting things done, getting his own way – these are important values in his world. He looks with contempt on his awkward, ineffectual son, someone so different from himself. A hard-drinking man who can be sardonic and cruel (e.g. p. 63, ll. 25 f.; p. 103, ll. 24 ff.), he only once appears vaguely proud of his son, when he believes that Larry is going out on a date with the neighbors' daughter. Carl is a typical 'good ol' boy' (cf. pp. 86 f. of this book) who looks down on everyone who doesn't share his attitudes. For example, he despises his brother-in-law for wearing a seat belt, which he regards as cowardly. (Ironically, he dies of a broken neck when his truck overturns – an accident he would have survived had his seat belt been fastened.) Evidently, he started an affair with their black housemaid Alice while his wife was pregnant with Larry, resulting in Alice's leaving the family and a latent conflict between Carl and his wife.

Ina Ott: character traits

Ina Ott is in many ways the opposite of her husband: soft-spoken, altruistic, pious. Her time is divided between housekeeping and volunteer work for the church. Larry's chronic illnesses have evidently occupied much of her attention and may have contributed to the estrangement between husband and wife. Ina is far too attached to her only child to raise him properly. She lavishes praise on him (p. 101, ll. 5 f.) instead of helping him to see himself realistically and speaks up for Larry's interests even when he is more than old enough to speak for himself. Her advice to Larry before his first date (p. 140, ll. 5–14) shows how out of contact with reality she is.

Her marriage functions mainly because Carl stays away from the house as much as possible and avoids discussions with his wife and son. The brief time they spend together at the dinner table is highly ritualized, with the mother watching over the behavior of her menfolk.

Carl's affair with Alice Jones

Carl Ott's affair with the housemaid stands between husband and wife like a ghost from the past, invisible but nonetheless present. It becomes clear when Ina stops her husband from driving Larry to school that she knows who the black woman and her son are. In the following months, she is privately angry at her husband for keeping his former mistress on their land, probably suspecting that Carl has taken up with Alice again. The depth of their estrangement becomes evident when Carl lambastes Larry over the missing rifle. Ina is furious that Alice is still living on their land and threatens to leave her husband if the black woman doesn't move elsewhere (p. 98, l. 33–p. 100, l. 19). Her repeated injunctions (*'Carl … Carl …'*) imply that her husband is breaking a tacit rule by referring openly to *'Silas that nigger boy'* (p. 99, l. 13), who is, as both know, his son. Carl taunts his wife by suggesting they could invite the boy and his mother to

Sunday dinner (p. 99, ll. 22 f.). Ultimately, the couple find no words to communicate what they feel, and Carl leaves the house.

Points to remember:

- The relationship between Carl Ott and his wife Ina is strained, partly because of Carl's affair with Alice Jones, partly because of their differing characters and interests.
- Larry suffers from the consequences of their opposing attitudes to him.

Alice Jones

Silas's mother appears as an active participant in the plot only in Chapter Six, where we see something of her character. Alice is described as being an attractive woman, even *'beautiful'* (p. 124, l. 14). In difficult situations (for example, when her boyfriend is arrested or when she is stranded in Mississippi with only the money in her handbag) she shows that she knows what she wants and how to get it. On the other hand, she is also a product of her upbringing: she knows that African Americans don't have the same rights as white Americans, that they can only survive if they 'play by the rules', and that incautious behavior can have deadly consequences (p. 230, ll. 2–6). She is against the friendship between Larry and Silas (p. 89, ll. 2–19), and she pleads with Silas to end his affair with Cindy, not because she has racist prejudices, but because she knows that there are still lots of white racists around who could take revenge on a black boy for crossing the color line. In Larry's case she also wants to keep her son from finding out who his father is. Alice's attitudes

Lacking a man she can depend on, Alice invests all her emotion in her son Silas (p. 230, l. 10). Silas is unable to cope with her emotional dependence on him, and later punishes her by withdrawal (p. 177, ll. 22 ff.), refusing to recognize that she is *'starving from loneliness'* (p. 178, l. 4).

In the end, she dies alone and lonely – presumably of a broken heart (p. 222, ll. 3 f.)

Wallace Stringfellow

Wallace and Larry: parallels

In some ways, Wallace Stringfellow is Larry's 'little dopplegänger', a weird loner and outsider who secretly hungers for companionship. While he is lying in hospital recovering from his gunshot wounds, Larry reflects on his relationship to Wallace and realizes that Wallace was in some ways like him: *'Larry saw a little of himself in him, maybe. This strange lonely kid. Maybe, to this kid, in this world Larry hadn't caught up to, Larry was even a kind of hero.'* (p. 264, ll. 28 ff.). Wallace also shares Larry's fascination with snakes. When he breaks into Larry's house and puts on Larry's zombie mask, he is playing the same role that Larry had played with him ten years before. Like Larry, Wallace is a high-school dropout and has no real job. A friendless loner, he suffers from low self-esteem, like Larry and Silas (p. 264, l. 2: *'I ain't worth a shit'*).

Wallace and Larry: important differences

But in other ways Wallace Stringfellow is in a category of his own. While Larry is unsparingly honest and straightforward, Stringfellow is a snoop and a liar. Larry is a harmless bookworm who stumbles into a situation he can't cope with and is wrongly branded a rapist and murderer. Stringfellow, on the other hand, is genuinely disturbed. In addition to his high consumption of alcohol and drugs, he has named his dog after a convicted serial murderer and indulges in abnormal sexual fantasies in volving enslavement and violence. His ex-girlfriend Evelyn claims that he tried to rape her (p. 256, ll. 17–26). During one of his visits to Larry it becomes obvious that Stringfellow believes that Larry raped and murdered Cindy and wants him to tell him all about it. When Larry stubbornly maintains his innocence, Stringfellow gives free rein to his perverse fantasies, talking himself into sexual arousal. When Larry turns his back on him, Stringfellow feels he has been betrayed and flies into a rage.

What brings these two outsiders together is not their repressed darker side, as Stringfellow believes, but rather their unfulfilled need for human companionship. Stringfellow mistakenly believes that Larry will understand him and his desires and feels cheated when he doesn't. Larry, desperately lonely as he is, comes to understand that his need for friendship led him to protect Stringfellow when he should have reported him to the police (p. 264, ll. 18–25).

Roy French

Roy French, a former game warden and Vietnam vet, is a white man in his late fifties and Silas's direct superior. He is often described as wearing a T-shirt with an aggressive, anti-gun control message. French himself, however, does not make an overly strict impression. He is generally good-humored, makes little jokes with Silas and allows Silas to adopt the same tone with him (e.g. p. 70, ll. 10–19). When they are on duty together, he is the one who gives the orders (for example, at Larry's house after the shooting, p. 76, ll. 16–29). Near the end of the story, French steps out of character for a moment to give Larry some personal advice (p. 280, ll. 29 f.). His occasionally gruff humor is possibly just his way of keeping people at a distance (e.g. p. 290, ll. 16–19), as his job occasionally requires him to perform unpleasant tasks (e.g. p. 211, ll. 3 ff.).

Angie Baker

'Angie' is probably short for 'Angela' – angel, which comes close to describing the role Angie plays in the novel. She is Silas's good angel, who looks after him when he is injured and tries to persuade him to accompany her to church. She is also the person who finds Larry when he is severely wounded and saves his life. Later she comes to the hospital and tells Larry that he would be welcome at the Baptist church she regularly attends. She is deeply attached to Silas and accepts him as he is, in spite of his shortcomings. Silas perhaps underrates the depth of her love and fears that she might leave him if she knew the truth about him (p. 214, ll. 3–6).

Cecil Walker

Cecil Walker is the stepfather of Cindy Walker, suggesting that he is the second (or third) husband of his wife. After suffering a back injury while working at the sawmill he was laid off and hasn't worked since then. Cecil is about the same age as Carl Ott, who appears to be his best friend; Carl and his wife evidently both knew Cecil when they were younger. Cecil has a reputation for doing 'crazy' things which generally display a rash, immature character. He began drinking heavily while still a teenager, and now spends most of his time sitting at home with a bottle in his hand. His stepdaughter Cindy despises him and accuses him of sexually molesting her. He can be cruel and violent, especially to younger people who can't defend themselves – people like Larry and Cindy.

Cindy Walker

Cindy Walker is sixteen when she falls in love with Silas Jones. She lives in a very isolated area with her mother and her mother's husband. Cindy is headstrong and independent for her age: she drinks, smokes, and evidently chooses her boyfriends herself without regard to their skin color. When a white motorist sees her walking down the road with Silas and asks if she needs help, she makes an obscene gesture and insults him (p. 227, l. 23). She feels cooped up in the tiny village where they live, constantly threatened by her brutal and predatory stepfather, and dreams of escape to someplace like Chicago, where they have real theatres (p. 227, ll. 11–17). When her stepfather gets wind of her clandestine relationship he drastically curtails her freedom; Cindy rebels and makes an escape plan, which, however, tragically backfires.

The Setting

The novel is set mainly in Chabot, a tiny hamlet of ca. 500 residents located somewhere in southern Mississippi. Chabot has a town hall with two employees, the town clerk (Voncille Bradford) and the police constable (Silas Jones). The part-time mayor (Morris Sheffield) is also a real-estate agent. There are a handful of businesses in the town, two of them on the border of bankruptcy due to the opening of a Wal-Mart (a huge American discounter) in Fulsom, the nearby county seat. Chabot has a middle school (grades 6–8) but no high school. In general, the town appears to be in a state of decline. Two office buildings are abandoned; there is no barber, no pharmacy, no ATM; cell phones only work some of the time. Silas's police car is thirty years old. Crime has apparently never been a major problem until very recently (Silas has never used his gun or Taser), but drug abuse is (cf. p. 21, l. 2 f.; p. 26, l. 31; p. 78, l. 4). Moreover, Chabot, like all towns in Gerald County, has a problem with alcohol abuse because it is the only county in the region in which alcoholic beverages are sold (cf. p. 27, ll. 7 f.).

The only employer of significance is the Rutherford Lumber Mill. Much of the surrounding land, wetland suitable only for growing evergreen trees, belongs to the Rutherford family. Since the Rutherfords more or less finance the community, they have tremendous influence.

In some ways, their status resembles that of feudal barons or landed gentry in earlier times. They protect their lands with fences and warning signs to ward off poachers (p. 36, ll. 16 ff.); on special occasions they invite selected guests to go on hunting expeditions (p. 15, l. 25–p. 16, l. 1). When their daughter is abducted, every available police officer in the area is put on alert (p. 21, ll. 16 ff.).

In the middle of Chabot society are what might be called the 'respectable' people, those who have regular work and families. At the time the story begins (c. 2007) this class includes both black and white. Three decades earlier, these two groups lived strictly segregated, and relations between them were frequently characterized by thinly-veiled hostility and racism (as Larry learns at Chabot Middle School, where black students are in the majority). In the present, blacks and whites in Chabot appear to mingle with little difficulty, often working together as colleagues (e.g. Silas and French, Angie and Tab), frequenting the same bars and diners.

At the bottom of the social ladder is a class of white people often derogatively labelled 'poor white trash'. In Chapter Two, the narrator paints a vivid portrait of the squalor and confusion they live in, even describing the road as '*White Trash Ave.*' (p. 36, l. 11–p. 37, l. 16). These people are mostly the chronically unemployed, alcoholics and drug addicts, young women who drift in and out of marriage, people with little education and no ambition. Wallace Stringfellow, a high-school dropout who lives on occasional jobs, presumably to finance his beer and marijuana consumption, could be reckoned among them, even though he doesn't live there. Traditionally, these people tend to be vicious racists, their skin color being their only claim to social status.

Narrative Structure

Crooked Letter, Crooked Letter has a relatively complex narrative structure that can make understanding the novel challenging. However, when you realize that it is based on two simple principles, the organization of the novel becomes clearer:

- The narrative perspective alternates between Larry Ott and Silas Jones; i.e. the odd-numbered chapters are told from Larry's point of view (but not by Larry), and the even-numbered chapters from Silas's viewpoint. (Chapter 19 is an exception: it alternates between Larry's and Silas's points of view.)
- The narrative alternates between the events of the present (presumably September 2007) and flashbacks to the past concentrating on the years 1979–1982.

The table below presents the events of the novel in a condensed form, showing their relationship in time:

chapter	present action	past action (flashbacks)
1	Larry is shot by Wallace Stringfellow.	
2	Silas finds M&M's body and kills a rattlesnake in a mailbox; Larry is found severely injured.	Silas recalls Larry's attempts to contact him two years earlier.
3		Larry's childhood: his father's workshop; bad experiences at school (6th grade); first contact with Silas and his mother (8th grade, 1979); friendship.

4	Silas goes to Larry's house, meets French, looks for clues.	
5		Summer after 8th grade: Larry and Silas go to Walkers' house; Carl Ott makes his sons fight; end of friendship.
6	Silas goes back to Larry's house, discovers a photo of his mother.	Silas recalls his earlier life in Chicago and their move to Chabot.
7		1982: Larry's 'date' with Cindy W. and the aftermath, leading up to c. 2005.
8	Silas tells Angie about his former relationship to Larry; visits Larry and his mother; stops Stringfellow on a private road; goes back to cabin, discovers grave.	Silas recalls the only time he visited Larry at home and cut the grass.
9		Stringfellow's visits to Larry (2007).
10	Tina Rutherford is found dead; funeral; Silas talks to Mrs. Ott about his mother, tells Angie about his relationship with Cindy W.	Silas recalls his affair with Cindy (1982).
11	Larry regains consciousness; French tries to persuade him to confess.	

12	Silas tells French about his connection with Cindy; tries to get information from Larry; learns that Stringfellow has snakes and can get violent.	
13	Larry lies alone in his room zapping through the TV channels.	Larry recalls Stringfellow's last visit, when he confessed to having 'done something'.
14	Silas goes to Stringfellow's place; gunfight.	
15	Larry tells French about Stringfellow.	
16	Silas and Larry talk.	
17	Silas is discharged from hospital.	
18	Silas moves in with Angie; go to Larry's house to prepare for Larry's discharge.	
19	Larry leaves hospital on his own; Silas finds him and drives him home.	

The author uses slightly different techniques for his two main characters: Silas is able to recall events from his past, and sometimes he recounts them to others (Angie, French). In such cases (as in Chapter 10) the author uses a mixture of direct speech and flashback to integrate events of the past into the narrative. In the case of Larry Ott, this is not possible, as Larry is in a coma after the shooting (Chapter 1) until he regains consciousness (Chapter 11). For this reason, the flashbacks relating to Larry are integrated directly into the narrative. Usually the narrator provides the reader with a time reference in the opening sentences of the chapter (*'It was just after dawn in March 1979'*; *'It was 1982'*; *'When he was thirty-one years old [...]'*).

As mentioned above, the events of the plot are related alternately from Larry's and Silas's points of view. That means that we, the readers, only see, experience and know what Larry or Silas sees, experiences and knows (unless, of course, another character recounts an experience in direct speech). Franklin uses different narrative techniques to achieve this effect:

- Point-of-view narration: *'The first thing he noticed was that they didn't have coats'* (p. 44, l. 1). Chapter Three begins inside Larry's head, looking out into the world through his eyes. The pronominal references (*he*, *they*) are not explained, as they are self-evident to Larry's consciousness. In this way the narrator creates the illusion that Larry's consciousness is *his* consciousness, separated only by the choice of personal pronoun (*he* instead of *I*).
- Indirect thought: *'He wondered what they were doing here, this far out, before the store opened'* (p. 44, ll. 12 f.). We learn what Larry is thinking, but his thoughts are expressed indirectly, not in the form of direct speech ('What are they doing out here, this far out, before the store opens?' Larry wondered).
- Implicit indirect thought: *'Larry stuck out his calfskin glove. Silas's slender brown hand was bare, and despite the quick soul shake it gave, Larry felt how cold his skin was. If he gave him one of his gloves, they could each have one warm hand. He wanted to do this, but how?'* (p. 45, ll. 11 ff.). The final two sentences are in fact thoughts that are going through Larry's head. The narrator, however, does not explicitly label them as such ('Larry tried to figure out how he could ...'). Instead, he expects us, the readers, to recognize that we are witnessing the events of the plot as they are reflected in Larry's (or Silas's) consciousness. For this reason, the entire text of the novel is saturated with subjectivity, dealing as it does with two adult men confronting (and re-interpreting) the events of their past.

Genre

Franklin's novel *Crooked Letter, Crooked Letter* is first and foremost a **detective** or **crime novel**. The opening sentence makes clear to the reader that a crime has (presumably) taken place ('*The Rutherford girl had been missing for eight days* …'). As we read on, we learn that the main character, Larry Ott, is under police surveillance because of his past and is regarded as a suspect in the Rutherford case. Toward the end of the chapter, we learn that Larry was suspected of the abduction of another girl, Cindy Walker, 25 years earlier, but denies responsibility for her disappearance. Finally, he becomes the victim of yet another crime, committed by a masked assailant, before the chapter ends.

On the surface level, the plot deals with the efforts of the police to solve the two crimes mentioned in the first chapter (the earlier crime, the alleged abduction and murder of Cindy Walker, is left unsolved). Silas Jones, the local police constable, and his superior, Chief Inspector French, investigate the shooting of Larry Ott, who is also a prime suspect in the Rutherford case. They examine the scene of the crime (the Otts' house), collect clues, and interview witnesses. In the course of the novel, bits and pieces of information begin to fall together: somebody has put a rattlesnake in a woman's mailbox, Tina Rutherford's body is found buried in a cabin on Larry's land. In the end, suspicion falls on Wallace Stringfellow, who betrays himself by resisting arrest and committing suicide when cornered by the police. Larry awakes from his coma and reveals that Stringfellow was also the masked assailant. Larry's name is cleared, and the police conclude that not Larry, but the stepfather Cecil Walker was responsible for Cindy's death.

In some ways, the reader is put in the position of the detective: in the even-numbered chapters, we accompany Silas on his daily rounds as he searches for clues. At the same time, we are better informed than Silas, as we are also given access to information he lacks, information that comes from Larry Ott (in the odd-numbered chapters). For instance, we are witnesses to Stringfellow's perverse fantasies and violent behavior (Chapter Nine) long before Larry is able to tell the police about his suspicions. In this way, the reader has a broader overview of the facts of the case than the official investigators – a perspective that can heighten the suspense, as for example in Chapter Fourteen, when the reader (unlike the protagonist) knows that Silas is about to confront a dangerous psychopath.

Trouble spot: *Spannung*

The German word *Spannung* has two English equivalents, both of which are relevant for the novel at hand:
suspense is the feeling that something dramatic is about to happen, i.e. the story becomes *suspenseful* (Ger. *spannend*);
tension describes the general atmosphere of a situation or a personal relationship and is the opposite of *relaxed* or *harmonious*. For example, we see in Chapter Five that the relationship between Larry's parents is *tense* (Ger. *angespannt*).

But *Crooked Letter, Crooked Letter* is more than just a 'whodunit'. Franklin paints a vivid portrait of a small Southern town struggling to cope with economic depression, rapid change and the burdens of the past. In many ways, Franklin's novel fits a genre known as **Southern Gothic**. The term Southern Gothic refers back to Gothic fiction, a genre of European and American fiction that became popular in the 19th century. Gothic fiction, in some ways a further development of Romanticism, emphasized the irrational and supernatural at the expense of the mundane and bourgeois. Famous works include Mary Shelley's *Frankenstein* (1818), Emily Brontë's *Wuthering Heights* (1847), and the stories of E.T.A. Hoffmann and Edgar Allan Poe. Southern Gothic fiction, which emerged in the 1930s, concentrates on the morbid side of life in the South. Typical themes are madness and suicide, incest, alcoholism, forbidden interracial love and the burdens of heredity. Where Gothic literature uses crumbling manor houses and castles as the chilling setting for the plot, Southern Gothic features decaying mansions and inbred rural communities. The strictly ordered caste system of the South (white landowners – townspeople – poor whites – blacks), which had more in common with the class system of 19th century Europe than with the society of New York or Boston of that time, lent itself readily to the Gothic genre. But unlike Gothic fiction, which aims mainly to produce an emotional effect, Southern Gothic literature critically explores the special character of a region and the values it represents.

Franklin's novel contains a number of elements typical of Southern Gothic, beginning with the setting, a tiny, decaying Mississippi backwater where everybody knows everybody else (or at least thinks they do). Behind the façade of tedium and predictability, dark passions are at work. Two girls disappear mysteriously, a corpse is discovered in a swamp, an eccentric recluse is found severely injured, a rattlesnake turns up in someone's mailbox. As we learn more about the characters, we see that several of them have something to hide. Like the two bodies that are uncovered in the course of the novel, the past inexorably rises to the surface and demands its tribute from the living. The most obvious example is that of Larry and Silas, who must come to terms, not only with the consequences of their abortive friendship, but also with the fact of their kinship. And of course, Franklin's intention is also typical of the genre. His tale of injustice and its aftereffects lays bare the hypocrisy and self-righteousness of a tight-knit, isolated community under pressure, even as the rapprochement between Larry and his black half-brother opens up the possibility of healing and atonement.

A number of the figures and character constellations in *Crooked Letter, Crooked Letter* have parallels in Harper Lee's classic novel *To Kill a Mockingbird* (1960). In several respects, Larry Ott resembles 'Boo' Radley, a harmless recluse ill-treated by his father, who is falsely stylized as a fearsome monster by the local children. Moreover, there are parallels between Cindy Walker and her alcoholic, shiftless stepfather and the McEwell family (father and daughter) in Lee's novel. In both stories, a white girl initiates an affair with a young black man and is savagely punished by her (step-)father. In both novels, the white male attempts (successfully) to shift the blame to someone else. These parallels should not be interpreted as evidence that Franklin 'borrowed' ideas for his novel from Lee; they simply demonstrate that there are common themes and interests that can be found in various works belonging to the genre.

Thematic Vocabulary: The Language of Crime and Detection

Every field of human activity has its own special vocabulary – crime is no exception. The words and phrases in the list below will help you to express yourself more precisely when talking or writing about a detective novel like *Crooked Letter, Crooked Letter*.

English	German equivalent	Usage example
accomplice	Komplize, -zin	Do you think he had an accomplice?
accuse sb. of sth.	jdm. etwas vorwerfen	He was accused of armed robbery.
the accused	der/die Angeklagte	The accused failed to appear in court.
alleged [ə'ledʒd]	mutmaßlich	the alleged murderer of Tina Rutherford
allegedly [ə'ledʒɪdli]	angeblich	Allegedly, he was at home all evening.
alibi ['æləbaɪ]	Alibi	Neither of them has an alibi for the time of the break-in.
case	Fall	The Walker case was closed years ago.
clue	Spur, Hinweis	The police searched the house for clues.
commit a crime	eine Straftat begehen	A murderer is someone who has committed a murder.
confess (to a crime)	(eine Straftat) zugeben	Has the accused confessed yet?

culprit, criminal, perpetrator	Verbrecher, -in/ Täter, -in	The police were under enormous pressure to find the culprit.
evidence *(uncountable)*	Indizien	Is there any evidence that Stringfellow was in Ott's house?
exonerate	entlasten	exonerating evidence
guilty ['gɪlti] guilt	schuldig Schuld	The court found him guilty of armed robbery.
incriminate	belasten, inkriminieren	incriminating evidence
innocent innocence	unschuldig Unschuld	People treat him like a criminal, even though he is innocent.
investigate a crime	in einer Strafsache ermitteln	The police are still investigating the shooting.
motive	Motiv	What was his motive for shooting Ott?
proof [pru:f] *(usually uncountable)*	Beweis	French is convinced of his guilt, but he hasn't got any proof.
prove [pru:v]	beweisen	He is certain that Larry is the murderer, but he has no way of proving it.
question (a witness, a suspect, etc.)	jdn. befragen	He questioned the bystanders, but no one had noticed anything suspicious.

scene of the crime	Tatort	The police thoroughly examined the scene of the crime.
solve a crime/ case	ein Verbrechen aufklären/einen Fall lösen	As the police could find no conclusive evidence, the case went unsolved.
suspect [sə'spekt] sb. (of sth.)	jdm. verdächtigen	French suspects Larry of having murdered two girls.
suspect ['sʌspekt]	Verdächtige(r)	Larry is the prime suspect in the Rutherford case.
suspicion [sə'spɪʃn]	Verdacht	Suspicion falls on Larry Ott, an outsider.
testify	aussagen (vor Gericht)	She knows it was her ex-husband, but will she testify against him in court?
testimony	Aussage (vor Gericht)	His ex-wife's testimony weakened his case.
witness (v)	(als Zeuge) beobachten	Did anyone witness the robbery?
witness (n)	Zeuge, -gin	I want you to interview the witnesses.

Language and Imagery

Franklin's language is rich in images that create a dense, emotionally charged atmosphere. This is especially evident in the descriptive passages that occur mainly in the earlier chapters of the novel. Examples:

Back in the Jeep, he cranked down his window and floated through identical pine trees, tall wet bitterweed in the middle of the road wiping the hood like brushes at a carwash. Where the land slanted down the trees had angled their trunks gracefully like arms bent at the elbow. (p. 16, ll. 21–25)

The underbrush thinned as he went, the air hotter, muggier, and suddenly the trees had thrown open their arms to a high white sky, a burst of glowing logs and schools of steaming toadstools and clouds of gnats, wet leaves sparkling like mirrors and a spiderweb's glowing wires. (p. 18, ll. 26–30)

similes and metaphors (→p. 92)

The similes ('*like brushes at a carwash*') and metaphors ('*the trees had thrown open their arms to a high white sky*'; which is also personification) are used to link the world of nature and the human world, reminding us that what we call civilization is intimately connected with the life of the non-human environment that surrounds us.

The style of the novel

Franklin's style varies between the terse style of detective stories, with short, sometimes fragmentary sentences, and a more ornate style that uses both enumerations and more complex parenthetic constructions, frequently in the form of participle phrases:

sentence fragment

enumeration

parenthetic insertion

Silas took off his hat. In the distance, three or four lumps in rags of plaid clothing, lodged in the water among a vista of cypress trees and knees and buzzards black and parliamentary and all the flies a world could need. A large shadow passed him and he looked overhead where more buzzards circled yet, some at near altitudes not colliding but seeming to pass through one another, their wings and tail feathers sun-silvered at the tips. His mouth was dry. (p. 19, l. 28–p. 20, l. 4)

with participle phrases

The symbols used in the novel are closely connected with the natural world. For one thing, the author reminds us constantly of the circle of **growth** and **decay**. This phenomenon is obvious in the South, where wooden buildings don't last long if they are neglected and new growth springs up overnight to cover yesterday's footsteps. Settings in the novel are frequently described as dying, decaying, overgrown with vegetation:

symbolism

growth and decay

Silas passed the Wal-Mart and then the arrowed sign to Fulsom's business district. Soon the road bottlenecked down to a two-lane and the businesses became sparse, the sidewalks cracked, sprouting weeds, buildings posted, windows and doors boarded. He passed what used to be a post office. He passed a clothing store that had gone so long without customers it'd briefly become a vintage clothing store without changing stock. Building on his right was an ex-Radio Shack, windows now busted or shot out and the roof fallen in so thoroughly the floor was shingled, the walls beginning to sag and buckle. The only businesses still open on this end were a cheap motel that catered to quickies and Mexican laborers and the garage he was approaching, OTTOMOTIVE REPAIR painted on the side in fading green letters. (p. 32, l. 26– p. 33, l. 7)

images of economic decline

Now, as he walked, slipping through leaves and vines and ivy and spiderwebs and arcs of briar, he noticed how different the land was, how quickly it could change, such a ragged jungle now, scarred with white deadfall, no longer the brief paradise two boys had had those years ago. […] Using his hat to rake down the briars, he was breathing hard and nearly bumped into the wall of the cabin before he saw it.

Smaller somehow, darker wood, more weathered. Vines and kudzu had nearly overtaken the place, it seemed the heart of some struggle, as if the vegetation were trying to claim the

Nature reclaims the abandoned cabin.

structure back into itself, pull it down, the earth suddenly an organic breathing mass underneath Silas, he could almost feel the friction, hear the viscous grumble of digestion. In front he eased up the steps, soft as moss, the porch like a cave, vegetation on all sides and bees boiling out of white blooms, live vines constricting dead ones, hanging from the roof. An enormous gray moth cupped to the wall. Gently, he moved coils of ivy aside and peered through the snakehead kudzu leaves to where the front door was secured with a rusty padlock. (p. 178, l. 8 – 179, l. 2)

Toward the end of the novel, the notion of decay reappears on a moral level, as Larry watches television in his hospital bed and realizes that the world outside has somehow lost its innocence in the 25 years he lived in isolation:

But watching its images, he was catching up to what the world had become. No more the world of green leaves where his father had carried a shotgun to school, left it in the corner by the woodstove, walking home shooting squirrels for dinner. Summers Carl Ott had gone shirtless and grown dark brown from the sun and found ticks in his hair and chiggers fattening with his blood. Now the land had been clear-cut. Mosquitoes infected you with West Nile and ticks gave you Lyme disease. The sun burned its cancer into your skin, and if you brought a gun to school it was to murder your classmates. (p. 264, l. 31–p. 265, l. 5)

contrast: then and now

a world in decay

Closely connected with the symbols of decay and renewal is the idea that the past is never really gone, that it merely lingers beneath the surface, waiting for its chance to come to light. In the words of CI French: *'[…] you can bury the past but it always seems to come back, one way or another'* (p. 243, ll. 5 f.). This notion forms a kind of **leitmotif** that appears in various forms throughout the novel, for example in the two corpses that are discovered (Chapter 2, p. 21; Chapter 10, p. 209). Both are murder

past and present

symbol: the dead reappear

victims; both bodies were buried in places where they would 'never' be found. And yet both come to light again, and the murderer must pay the price for his crimes. The motif of the 'walking dead' reappears in the zombie mask that plays a significant role in the story and in Cindy Walker's 'ghost' (even if it only exists in Silas's imagination; p. 294, ll. 24–31).

Franklin finds his most vivid image for an irrepressible past near the end of the novel:

When he left, Larry lay amid his machines, thinking of Silas, how time packs new years over the old ones but how those old years are still in there, like the earliest, tightest rings centering a tree, the most hidden, enclosed in darkness and shielded from weather. But then a saw screams in and the tree topples and the circles are stricken by the sun and the sap glistens and the stump is laid open for the world to see. (p. 280, l. 33–p. 281, l. 4)

the image of the tree of life

The tree grows, but its history forms its core, one that cannot be denied indefinitely. The metaphor applies most obviously to Silas, who represses the truth of his past for 25 years, pretends not to see, thinks things will work out on their own, then comes home again to find the past catching up with him: '*Here it all came. A quarter of a century bunching up on him, bearing down, a truck slamming on its brakes and its logs sliding forward, over the cab, through the window, the back of his head, shooting past him in the road*' (p. 248, ll. 10–13). In the end, (almost) all comes out, and Larry and Silas, '*like survivors of an explosion*' (p. 282, l. 9) are left to pick up the pieces of their lives and make a new start.

Silas: a repressed past catches up with him

There are a few other symbols of importance in the novel, for example, the rifle belonging to Carl Ott that Larry lends to Silas when they first meet in the woods but doesn't get back again until after he returns home from hospital. Originally a symbol of the friendship

symbol: the rifle

between Larry and Silas, it soon becomes an object of contention, then – like the bond between the two half-brothers – lies forgotten and ignored for 28 years until Silas takes it out and cleans it before bringing it back to the Otts' house, symbolically restoring order to their world.

symbol: the snake

A further symbol is the snake, most prominently connected with Wallace Stringfellow, who collects them (especially the poisonous ones) and presumably puts one of them in a mailbox to take deadly revenge on his ex-girlfriend. Like the snake, Stringfellow is crafty and devious, striking out unexpectedly when he sees his chance. It is probably not coincidental that a black snake appears on the road just before Larry sees Cindy Walker for the last time (p. 150, l. 7) and in the grass as Silas stands in front of the Walkers' empty house 25 years later (p. 294, l. 7). In both cases, the snake is connected with danger, either impending or in the past. (Larry is also connected with snakes, but this connection is mainly made by others; p. 164, ll. 17 f.; p. 167, ll. 6 f.).

symbol: the mask

Finally, Larry's monster mask can also be understood as a symbol. Wearing his zombie mask, Larry is allowed to stand in the limelight a brief hour (p. 165). In the role of monster, Larry is accepted, but when he takes the mask off and becomes Larry Ott again, '*just a hick that nobody liked*' (p. 164, l. 13), he is demonstratively ignored by the other students and wanders off into the night. After Cindy's disappearance, Larry is made a 'monster' by the community, who are convinced that he is a psychopath. Wallace Stringfellow, who feels the monster in his own soul, is attracted to Larry, mistakenly believing they have something in common. When Larry proves him wrong, Wallace reappears as the monster in the Otts' house and shoots him. '*Larry felt a strange forgiveness for him because all monsters were misunderstood*' (p. 14, ll. 18 ff.). Larry understands better than any other character in the story that the monster is just a mask, it is what the others (want to) see, and that behind it lies a desperate loneliness.

the title of the novel

Finally, the title of the novel can also be understood symbolically (the author's epigraph on p. 6 links the title superficially to the setting, and, in a broader sense, to the themes of childhood and education). Silas and Larry are both 'crooked' characters who have been 'bent' by fate. Like the letter S (and the river that gave its name to the state of Mississippi), their lives meander in seemingly random directions, pushed aside by the vagaries of circumstance. They both lack a clear direction in life and passively allow fate to take its course. It isn't until the end of the story that they re-converge and it becomes evident how closely their biographies parallel each other.

Themes

At the heart of Franklin's novel lies a dense cluster of themes involving the concepts of **identity, friendship, loyalty** and **guilt**. To a large extent, these themes are connected with the biographies of Larry and Silas; other characters (and the community as a whole) play a role too, but only a minor one.

core themes of the novel

In their early adolescence, when they first meet, Silas and Larry share certain identity problems. Larry is rejected by his cold father and coddled by his overprotective mother; with no siblings (that he knows of) and no friends, Larry has no male role model to help him discover his identity. Silas has a similar problem, although for different reasons. He is emotionally dependent on his struggling single mother, without the benefit of an older brother or other male relative. He was uprooted from his life in Chicago and taken to a region whose ways are foreign to him. Furthermore, he must deal with the 'colour line' that separates him from his white friend Larry and his white girlfriend Cindy.

Larry and Silas: shared identity problems

In spite of living in a seemingly intact family, Larry's isolation is more complete than Silas's. Physically and socially awkward, introverted and lacking in self-esteem, Larry has no real friends at school. His loneliness makes him desperate for acceptance, which leads him to indulge in unwise behavior such as insulting a black girl or giving Silas a rifle belonging to his father – in each case with drastic repercussions. The same urge to belong causes Larry to accept Cindy's offer of a date without question, with even more drastic consequences. And many years later, Larry allows Wallace Stringfellow to wheedle his way into his life, although he finds him repulsive, simply because Stringfellow is the first person in 25 years who treats him like a human being. It is Stringfellow who provides Larry with a new, dubious notion of friendship, meaning sharing one's dirty secrets without fear of be-

Larry's urge to belong

a false notion of friendship

trayal (p. 202, ll. 26–31). Lying in hospital, shot through the chest by his 'friend', Larry reflects that his longing for human companionship may have enticed him into accepting a false idea of loyalty (p. 264, ll. 18–25).

misplaced loyalty

The great exception in his life is the brief friendship with his half-brother Silas. Beyond the constraints of society, the white boy and the black boy share the simple pleasures of the wilderness, hunting and fishing in the nearby woods. But this episode is a *'brief paradise'* (p. 178, l. 11) that cannot last. When Carl Ott finds out what is going on, he forces the boys to fight, knowing in advance what the result will be. If the time the boys shared in the wilderness was the Garden of Eden, then the fight (with its ugly racial epithet) is the fall from grace. Larry knows that something in his world has changed and will never be the same again (p. 107, l. 8 ff.). The boys have betrayed their friendship by allowing their father to make enemies of them. After this incident, Larry's isolation is more complete than ever. In Silas's words, he becomes *'just a hick that nobody liked'* (p. 164, l. 13).

interracial friendship outside the bounds of society

Paradise lost

Larry and Silas betray their friendship.

Larry feels guilty for calling his only friend a 'nigger'; Silas forgets him, ignores him, goes off to college to play baseball. In the meantime, Larry has become an outcast in his community. In the tight-knit world of Chabot, the pressure to conform to accepted standards is enormous. Those who adhere to expectations belong; those who deviate from these expectations do not. When the community comes under pressure – Cindy Walker has disappeared under mysterious circumstances – people seek a scapegoat to explain the inexplicable and decide that Larry is the perpetrator (although there isn't a shred of evidence incriminating him). His 'weird' interests and deviant behavior are sufficient proof for them. The force of their ostracism is so great that no one is willing to have anything to do with him; a quarter of a century later people still make casual jokes about his psychopathic inclinations (p. 29, l. 7; p. 30, ll. 21 f.). And when another girl

the pressure to conform

Larry is made a scapegoat.

the power of ostracism

disappears, suspicion immediately falls on Larry once again. The influence of public opinion is so great that even someone as gentle and sensitive as Angie begins to imagine lines of development that could have led Larry to commit a brutal crime (p. 162, ll. 9–23). At this point, Silas realizes that he can no longer remain silent; he confesses his involvement in the Cindy Walker case to Angie, and with this confession he begins to face his guilt for turning his back on Larry, for ignoring his existence twenty-five long years when he could have exonerated him: *'You let him take the blame. All this time'* (p. 231, l. 31). For the first time, Silas assumes responsibility for his actions; he tracks down Larry's assailant, looks after Larry's mother (and his chickens), helps Angie to clean up Larry's house and even has satellite television installed. His injured left arm is a burden, but he thinks of the pain as *'penance'* (p. 294, l. 11) with which he atones for his guilt.

Silas confronts his guilt.

acts of atonement

Closely connected with the theme of guilt and atonement is that of **past and present** (→Language and imagery, p. 72). Both protagonists – Larry and Silas – are in a sense trapped in their past. Both are given a pseudo-identity by the community: Larry becomes 'Scary Larry', the neighborhood psychopath, Silas remains '32', star player of a bygone era. Larry can't prove that he is innocent; Silas fails to find the courage to admit his guilt. Confused and disoriented in their lives, both men suffer under the burden of the past, a burden that prevents them from living fulfilled, mature lives. The final chapters of the novel suggest that, now that the skeletons of the past have all come out of their closets, the way to a better future may lie open to them.

Larry and Silas: crippled by the burden of the past

Pseudo-identities replace real identity.

The American South

When Americans speak of the South, they usually mean a geographical region that extends from Virginia southwestward as far as Texas. This part of the country has its own history and culture going back to the beginning of European settlement. To understand what makes the South different from the Northeast or the Midwest, for example, you need to know something about American history.

The colonial era

Early European settlement in the southeastern part of North America was driven by agricultural investors interested in making a profit (for example, with tobacco or cotton). British merchants soon realized that huge profits could be made with the products that grew in the farming regions of the South with their hot summers and mild winters. When it was discovered that the climate was too hot for laborers from the British Isles, African slaves were bought from slave traders and transported by ship in large numbers to work on the plantations.

This development differed radically from that in the northern colonies, where religiously-inspired groups such as the Puritans and the Quakers founded settlements in which their communities could live in freedom and self-determination. Moreover, the influx of tradesmen, artisans and small independent farmers in the North created a society very different from the agricultural, slave-based economy of the South.

The Civil War (1861–1865)

After the colonies gained independence, the two parts of the nation continued to develop in radically different ways. While cities in the North grew into centers of industry and commerce, the South remained a region of small towns and sprawling plantations. Slowly opposition to slavery on moral grounds (= abolitionism) increased in the northern states. When Republican candidate Abraham Lincoln stated that he would limit slavery if elected president, the southern states threatened to leave the Union. Lincoln won the election of 1860, and eleven southern states declared themselves independent as the Confederate States of America. The federal government declared the move illegal, and the Civil War began. It ended in 1865, after more than 600,000 people had died. The slaves, who Lincoln had officially declared free in 1863, were now liberated in fact.

For the South, the Civil War ended in complete disaster. The governments of the eleven rebel states were dissolved, replaced by military governments that remained in power for the next twelve years ('Reconstruction'). The owners of large plantations handed over the administration of their land to so-called agents. These agents divided the lands into small plots that they rented to the former slaves on terms that made the agents rich and kept the black population poor ('sharecropping'). With no capital, no education and no tools, the blacks had little choice but to accept what was offered them. The collapse of the 'Old South' that had existed before the war led to an economic, political and social paralysis that lasted over a century.

The Jim Crow Era

After the fall of the Confederacy, African Americans living in the South became free citizens of the United States, but often on paper only. Laws were quickly passed that kept blacks from voting, for example. As time passed, whites and blacks continued to inhabit different worlds. Southern states had separate schools and churches for the two races; even water fountains and toilet facilities were separate ('segregation'). Around 1900, instances of lynching became increasingly common. The victim was almost always a young black male, his 'crime' generally involved a white girl or woman. In many cases it was enough for a rumor to start that so-and-so had 'approached' a white woman in a certain way to produce an angry mob willing to take justice into its own hands.

The phenomenon of lynching is closely linked to the deep-rooted hypocrisy underlying race (and gender) relations in the South. Traditionally, it was not uncommon for white slave owners to sexually exploit their female slaves. As years passed, generations of black and white Southerners emerged that were related to each other by blood. When, however, white women and black men felt attracted to each other, they risked incurring the wrath of white male society, which stopped at nothing in its hypocritical quest to defend 'the honor of the white race'.

The Civil Rights Movement

Beginning in the early 20th century, millions of black families left the South for what they hoped would be a better life in the North (the 'Great Migration'). For those who remained, segregation and fear

were a way of life. Things changed with the advent of television. For the first time, white Americans in other regions were able to see what happened when peaceful demonstrators were beaten by the police or attacked by police dogs. Presidents Kennedy and Johnson used their authority to end segregation and discrimination throughout the USA. In particular, guaranteed voting rights made it possible for southern blacks to actually exercise the political power they had been granted on paper a century earlier. The pathway to real change was laid.

The New South

Beginning in the late 1960s and 70s, a younger generation of political leaders (of mixed race and gender) began changing the face of southern politics. At the same time, the economic base of the South began to diversify, creating new jobs in the manufacturing and financial sectors. Workers and retired people alike flocked to the 'Sunbelt' states, and cities like Atlanta and Charlotte grew to become major centers of commerce and enterprise. Race relations have improved as well; in recent decades, there have been fewer race riots in the South than in other parts of the nation.

Southern exceptionalism

The remarkable progress in the South can't completely mask the fundamental differences that still remain between the two halves of the nation. For one thing, in spite of slavery, southern society was for a long time far more homogeneous than northern society. The millions of immigrants who poured into the USA in the latter 19th and early 20th century settled in the North and the Midwest; the rural South, with its underdeveloped agrarian economy, had little to offer them. For the same reason, religion in the South remained very traditional (and powerful): virtually every Southerner was either Presbyterian, Baptist or Methodist. In the North, the 'established' Protestant churches had to adapt to a changing society in which Catholics, Jews and non-believers all desired influence.

Moreover, it is only the South that has experienced the trauma of defeat and loss. While America in general basks in the consciousness of being the richest and most powerful nation on earth, Southerners know what it means to see their world crumble to ruins. This historical experience has produced a sensibility for the impermanence of things that runs like a melancholy creek through much of southern literature. Many southern writers – including some of the finest authors America has produced – have a keen sense of the close link between past and present. In the words of novelist William Faulkner: 'The past is never dead. It's not even past. All of us labor in webs spun long before we were born, webs of heredity and environment, of desire and consequence, of history and eternity. Haunted by wrong turns and roads not taken, we pursue images perceived as new but whose providence dates to the dim dramas of childhood, which are themselves but ripples of consequence echoing down the generations.'

Southern white culture

The characteristic homogeneity of southern society, the product of centuries of stagnation, led to the creation of a culture that strikes outsiders as being more rigid and conservative than, for example, that of the Northeast or the West Coast of the USA. Traces of this traditional, often formal etiquette can be found in Franklin's novel, for example when Larry addresses his father with 'sir' and his mother with 'ma'am' and is not allowed to leave the table without complimenting his mother on her cooking. Church attendance on Sunday is obligatory. Men's and women's roles are relatively conservative (at least in the middle class): the men work, the women are homemakers and do volunteer work for the church. 'Nice' girls don't have sex before marriage.

The reverse side of this rigidity is widespread hypocrisy: people find ways of getting around the rules that bind them. Carl Ott, bored and frustrated in his marriage to a woman who is so different from him, finds release in the 'men's club' atmosphere of his workshop and in an extramarital affair with his black housemaid. Cecil Walker molests his stepdaughter when his wife is at work, then denounces her as a 'whore'. The young women who populate 'White Trash Avenue', all in their early twenties, already have multiple marriages behind them. Early marriage and early divorce make it possible for them to avoid the public censure connected with casual sex. Drugs are illegal, but alcohol is easily available and widely consumed.

Because the South never had to incorporate large masses of 'newcomers', southern society tended to be tightly knit and intolerant of deviant behavior. Larry, a loner with unusual interests (reading), is immediately pegged as an outsider and treated accordingly. At school, his classmates either harass or ignore him. As an adult, Larry is caught in a vicious circle: because he is an outsider, he is groundlessly declared by public opinion to be the murderer of Cindy Walker, and because he is believed to be a murderer, he is ostracized, making him an outsider. Other 'outsiders' in southern society are homosexuals (cf. p. 201, l. 22) and Catholics (cf. p. 196, l. 4).

Among the 'insiders', one group deserves special attention. There is a certain type of southern white man popularly referred to as a 'good ol' boy'. A 'good ol' boy' is someone who conforms to accepted behavior, enjoys outdoor sports such as hunting, consumes alcohol, is patriotic, has the 'right' opinions and laughs at the 'right' things. Carl Ott and Cecil Walker both conform to this stereotype. Larry's Uncle Colin, on the other hand, does not. He is not aggressively masculine, does not appear to be athletically inclined, fastens his seat-belt, and is a vegetarian. Larry's similarity to this uncle alone would suffice to make him an untouchable for all the 'good ol' boys' of Chabot.

The 'good ol' boys' have their own special sense of humor that might strike outsiders as being a passive form of sadism. Misfortune that befalls others is a source of laughter to them, no matter who the victim is. Carl Ott even laughed when his own son was struck by a flying stone, then took a photo of the red mark on his stomach, later breaking out in laughter whenever he looked at the photo. The stories Carl and his friends laugh over invariably involve someone coming to harm. It is interesting to note that Silas, the poor black boy, doesn't find the story about Cecil throwing firecrackers at Cindy the least bit funny and calls his behavior 'mean'. Silas also risks his life by intervening on Cindy's behalf when Cecil tries to take her bath towel away, whereas Carl and Cecil find the whole business amusing.

Southern black culture

In general, the blacks in the story – like the whites – tend to stick to themselves and have their own forms of group solidarity (for example, Marla providing Silas with food for free). This holds true for their religious practice as well; even though the people of Chabot (both white and black) are mainly Baptists, they go to separate churches. At the time the story begins (presumably 2007), relations between black and white appear to be relatively relaxed; black and white colleagues work amicably side by side (e.g. Silas and French). In his dealings with white people as police constable Silas is never confronted with racial prejudice. This differs sharply from the impression we are given of life in the late 1970s, where there is little contact and considerable hostility between black and white. At Chabot Middle School, the black majority gangs up on helpless members of the white minority; Carl Ott and his cronies at the garage laugh at anecdotes about the crazy 'niggers'. In this respect, southern society has made tremendous progress.

Timeline: The American South

1607	The first permanent British settlement in North America is established at Jamestown, Virginia.
1619	The first African slaves are brought by Dutch traders to work in Jamestown.
1781	The 13 American colonies become the independent United States of America. Slavery is legal in the southern colonies, but illegal in the northern ones.
1861–1865	The Civil War breaks out between the Union (= northern and mid-western states) and the Confederacy (= eleven southern states). The war ends with widespread destruction in the South. Slavery is abolished.
1865–1877	Reconstruction: the former Confederate states are ruled by military governments under direct supervision of the federal government in Washington.
1877–ca. 1955	The 'Jim Crow' Era: dubious laws enforce segregation and deny African Americans in the South equal access to education, employment and voting rights.
ca. 1910–1970	The 'Great Migration': c. 6 million African Americans leave the rural South and move to the urban centers of the North, the Midwest and California.

1955	Emmett Till, a 14-year-old black boy from Chicago, is brutally murdered in Mississippi for allegedly whistling at a white woman. The Civil Rights Movement begins with the Montgomery (Alabama) bus boycott, led by Martin Luther King, Jr.
1964/65	Congress passes the Civil Rights Act and the Voting Rights Act, two landmarks on the way to racial equality. Violence is widespread in the South as white racists (sometimes with police support) try to prevent blacks from exercising their rights. Three young activists from the North are murdered in Mississippi.
1970s onward	As a result of civil rights legislation, massive shifts take place in the political landscape of the South. The 'New South' emerges as industries move to the 'Sunbelt states', revitalizing the economy of the long-stagnant region.
1972	Andrew Young is elected to the House of Representatives from Georgia. Young is the first African American to be elected to Congress from a former Confederate state in the 20th century.
1989	Douglas Wilder is elected governor of Virginia, the first African-American governor of a southern state since Reconstruction.
1996	Atlanta (Georgia) hosts the Summer Olympics.

School, Sports and Racial Integration

Sports play a far larger role at American high schools than at most schools in Germany. The main reason is that there are no sports clubs (in the German sense of the word) in the USA. That means that if you play a sport, you play at and for your school. School teams play in regional leagues against the teams of other high schools. Because the 'honor' of the school is at stake, especially where popular sports (baseball, football, basketball) are involved, schools traditionally invest a relatively large effort (marching band, cheerleaders, mascots, sponsors, etc.) in making sports competitions a major event. In many small towns in the US, school sports events are in fact the main source of live entertainment. Successful high-school athletes are among the most popular students at their school (and have the prettiest cheerleaders for their girlfriends). Conversely, students (like Larry in the novel) who are disinterested or useless at sports are generally treated as outsiders.

A similar system prevails at American colleges (including elite Ivy League institutions such as Yale and Harvard). Putting together a successful team is considered an important goal by university administrators. Many colleges and universities send 'scouts' to high-school matches to spot promising athletes, who may then be actively recruited by the college. If the student's parents are unable to finance four years of undergraduate study, the student is offered a 'scholarship' (= stipend). Such students are not explicitly required to play on the varsity team (as it is called), but it is tacitly assumed that they will. Moreover, they are required to maintain minimum academic standards alongside their sports careers.

In the novel *Crooked Letter, Crooked Letter*, Silas Jones (and to a lesser extent, Morton Morrisette) illustrates the two sides of institutionalized sports in the USA. Silas's talent at baseball makes him a high-school hero and paves the way for his admission to college. Presumably Silas was singled out and recruited for the University of Mississippi baseball team well before graduation from high school, in spite of his lackluster grades. He leaves Chabot during his junior year and spends his senior year at Oxford High School, where there are better opportunities for athletic training (p. 231, l. 21 ff.). After a serious accident ends his dream of a professional career, he is simply forgotten and left to fend for himself. Morrisette fares worse; after graduation from high school his career comes to an abrupt end, as there is no opportunity for him to play sports without an affiliation with a school or college. The fact that in their home town they are still referred to by their team nicknames, 'M&M' and '32', not by their given names, reflects how their identity still derives from the faded glory of their youth.

The recruitment and active promotion of 'scholar-athletes', disproportionally many of whom are African Americans, has sometimes led to controversy. Critics accuse university leaders of employing a double standard for admissions decisions, one for the athletically gifted and one for everybody else. When, for example, Harvard University created a Department of African-American Studies in the early 1970s, conservative white students acidly joked that its real purpose was to give the basketball team a subject they could understand. The true story is, of course, more complicated than this, but it cannot be completely denied that the pursuit of prestige in college athletics sometimes leads to exploitation and disregard for the fate of the individual.

Sports have played a key role in promoting racial integration in the USA. The exceptional talent of many African-American athletes went to waste as long as racial barriers prevented them from taking part in major-league sports. Pioneers like Jesse Owens (who won four gold medals at the 1936 Summer Olympics in Berlin), Joe Louis (world heavyweight boxing champion from 1937 to 1949), and Jackie Robinson (who became the first African-American player on a major-league baseball team in 1947) destroyed the myth of white superiority and paved the way for younger generations of gifted African-American athletes. Today, many sports would be unthinkable without them.

Glossary of Literary Terms

Allusion: a reference to a literary, cultural or historical source.
Atmosphere: the feeling or mood produced in a literary text created by the description of the setting, the landscape etc. (cf. p. xx of this book)

Characters

Round character: round characters develop in the course of the action and change their attitudes and values in response to what they experience during the story. The change of attitude is often brought about by a conflict or problem the character is confronted with. Both Larry and Silas are round characters.
Flat character: flat characters do not develop in the course of the action. They are usually the personification of a single idea or quality. Minor characters in a novel are often designed as flat characters that serve as a background or foil against which the round characters can be judged. Wallace Stringfellow is a flat character.

Imagery

Image: a word or series of words used by the author to appeal to the reader's imagination. An image is intended to bring a new feeling or a new perception to an object. The writer may appeal to any of the five senses or the sense of movement to enable the reader to perceive an object. Many images are conveyed by figurative language, especially by metaphors and similes.
Symbol: an element of imagery in which a concrete object represents not only itself, but also an abstract idea. For example, a red rose is a traditional symbol of love.
Metaphor: an element of imagery in which two seemingly dissimilar things are linked to each other in the form of an implicit comparison. The strength of a metaphor is its ability to convey a new and quite different feeling to the literal meaning of a word. Metaphor differs from simile in that it says that something is something else, while simile says that something is like something else.
Simile: an element of imagery in which two seemingly dissimilar things are linked to each other in the form of an explicit comparison

through the words 'like' or 'as'. A simile serves to offer the reader some new insight into the object under discussion. Simile differs from metaphor in that it says that something is like something else, while metaphor says that something is something else.

Motif: an image, phrase, idea etc. that plays an important role in a book, play, film etc. A motif that is used repeatedly is also called a leitmotif (pl. leitmotifs).

Narration

First-person narrator: a first-person narrator is a character in a story who tells the story. A first-person narrator usually has a limited point of view.

Third-person narration: the narrator of a text told in the third person may be either an omniscient narrator (who tells the story from different perspectives and angles and has an unlimited point of view) or a narrator with a limited point of view, usually that of one character of the story.

Flashback: an individual scene or event that took place before the present action in a story, film or novel.

Foreshadowing: the technique of hinting that something will take place in the future.

Theme: the central idea or topic in a novel, play etc.

Tone: the general attitude or feeling of a narrator expressed in a fictional

work toward the theme, a character etc. For example, the tone of the story can be humorous, ironic or solemn.

Written Test

At some point while working with *Crooked Letter, Crooked Letter* you will probably have to do a written test. What the test looks like depends to some extent on the *Bundesland* you are in. The following model exam is based on the type of written examination used in Baden-Württemberg.

Test

Text

From: Melinda D. Anderson, "When Black and White Children Grow Apart", *The Atlantic*, 14 June 2016

The image of black and white children hand-in-hand is possibly the most well-known and most often quoted line from Martin Luther King Jr.'s "I Have a Dream" speech. Over the years, black and white youngsters playing together has evolved from a civil-rights leader's vision of racial equality to a clothing retailer's marketing campaign, and in the process spawned a cultural meme – signaling everything from innocence and hope to a world free of interpersonal racism. Yet black and white childhood friendships, an inspiring notion, rarely happen organically.

According to a new study of elementary- and middle-school students, teacher behaviors may shape how students select and maintain friends and affect the longevity of interracial friendships. The study, led by researchers with New York University's Steinhardt School, finds that as students move through a single school year, from the fall through the spring semester, their number of cross-racial friendships decreases. What's more, students' perceptions of their teachers – who may treat children in the same class differently, for example – influenced the rate of growth in same-race friendships from the fall to the spring.

Elise Cappella, an associate professor of applied psychology at NYU and the study's lead author, said the group started out with a common understanding, supported by popular wisdom and established research, that as young people approach and enter adolescence, their likelihood of forming friendships across racial and ethnic groups decreases. […]

As the argument goes and studies prove, children of all backgrounds benefit from diversified classrooms and schools where they can interact with peers of different races and ethnicities. Teaching Tolerance, an educational project of the Southern Poverty Law Center, concluded in a comprehensive review of research on racial and ethnic diversity in schools that "a racially integrated student body is necessary to obtain cross-racial understanding, which may lead to a reduction of harmful stereotypes and bias." But access to diversity is only the first step, not the destination, said Cappella, noting that the study points to the need for teachers to create classrooms where interracial friendships can develop and grow.

The influence of teachers on students' cross-racial bonds manifests itself in two key ways. Researchers found smaller increases in same-race friendships from the fall to the spring in classrooms where student perceptions of teachers' warmth, respect, and trust – "My teacher pays attention to my feelings" and "My teacher helps children feel good about themselves" – were rated highest. And black children were more likely to make friends with white classmates during the school year in classrooms where teachers received high rankings on differential treatment – the survey asked children to rate their teacher's behavior toward a hypothetical high- or low-achieving peer. […]

Jennifer Orr, a white elementary-school teacher in northern Virginia, said she was fascinated on a personal and professional level by the study's analysis. Her oldest daughter, now in seventh grade, attended Annandale Terrace Elementary, a highly diverse school, from grades kindergarten through 5. "Her close circle [of friends] included a Korean girl, a few Latino girls and boys, and at least one girl from the Middle East, [but] she has only kept up with two friends from there: another white girl and a white boy." As a parent, Orr offered a caveat to the study's findings, bringing the role of parents into the picture. "The immediate thing that came to my mind … was how much parents may play a role" with race or ethnicity shaping how parents arrange get-togethers outside of school that can "deepen friendships while allowing others to flounder."

From her vantage point as a former teacher at Annandale Terrace for 16 years, Orr said she strived to create a classroom environment that fostered friendships across races and ethnicities through activities and lessons. When assigning class projects she encouraged diverse groupings of fourth- and fifth-graders to solidify existing friendships, adding "that's what strikes me the most from this study: The idea that friendships narrow during this age range." Orr also turned to literature, using books with interracial friendships "to help kids see these friendships as normal and good."

Annotations

5 clothing retailer: *Einzelhändler der Bekleidungsbranche* **6** spawn sth.: produce sth. **6** cultural meme: image that becomes popular via the internet and is often copied **9** organically: without outside help **12** longevity: *Langlebigkeit* **31** student body: *Schülerschaft* **37** manifests itself: becomes evident **44** differential treatment: treating students differently based on their ability **46** hypothetical: imaginary **55** caveat (Latin): word of caution **59** flounder: fail to develop **60** vantage point: *Blickwinkel*

Part A: Reading comprehension

1 The image of mixed-race children playing together *(choose one)*
A was created by the advertising industry.
B inspired a famous speech by Martin Luther King Jr.
C symbolizes the hope of a world without racism.
D has no connection with present-day reality.

2 The behavior of the teacher had no effect on student friendships. (*true/false*)
Evidence: ______________________

3 In the study described in the article, the number of interracial friendships declined in the course of the school year. (*true/false*)
Evidence: ______________________

4 The people who conducted the study assumed that young people entering adolescence would be more likely than others to form interracial friendships. (*true/false*)
Evidence: ____________________

5 A racially diverse student body *(choose two)*
A has a greater impact on student attitudes than teachers' behavior.
B is a necessary basis for teaching tolerance and understanding.
C benefits some minority groups more than others.
D can help prevent stereotyped thinking.
E doesn't always lead to interracial understanding.

6 Jennifer Orr's oldest daughter *(choose one)*
A had only white friends while at elementary school.
B had only non-white friends while at elementary school.
C attended an elementary school with a very mixed student body.
D blamed her mother for not inviting her non-white friends to her house.

7 Orr thinks that parents ____________________. *(complete)*

8 Name two classroom measures that Orr adopted to promote interracial friendships:
A ____________________
B ____________________.

Part B: Writing

1 Compare the conditions for the formation of interracial friendships as described in the text with the relations between black and white students at Chabot Middle School (*Crooked Letter, Crooked Letter*, Chapter Three).

2 Jennifer Orr believes that literature dealing with interracial friendship can positively influence students. Comment on this belief, referring to *Crooked Letter, Crooked Letter* as an example.

Dealing with the tasks

Part A: Reading comprehension

No matter which *Bundesland* you live in, you are probably familiar with closed and semi-closed test formats from listening comprehension tests. Typical task formats include:

- multiple choice
- true/false
- matching
- sentence completion/table completion/short answers.

Here are some general tips you should know:

- Read each task carefully. In the case of multiple choice tasks, for example, make sure you know how many answers to mark. (If you mark more answers than you are allowed to, you will receive no credit.)
- Answer every question, even if you are not sure. You will be given a point for each correct solution; there is no penalty for a wrong answer. So always make an intelligent guess if you don't know the right answer.
- Do the tasks in the given order, which as a rule corresponds to the order of the information in the text.
- If you are asked to supply evidence to support your answer, write down the line number(s) plus the first three and the last three words of the quote from the text that shows that your answer is correct (e.g. ll. 33–36, '*But access to … develop and grow*').
- Semi-closed tasks are ones in which you are asked to write down a short answer or to complete a statement in a few words. In such tasks, only the content matters, i.e. spelling and grammar mistakes don't count. Do not write down more answers than the task requires you to; if you do, you will receive no credit for the task, even if some of your answers are correct.

Tips on the tasks:

Task 1: All four answers contain ideas that can be found in the opening paragraph of the text. But three of them express them in a way that is false or not justified by the text. Read all four answers carefully, looking for possible mistakes. Rule out the completions that you think are obviously wrong, then compare the remaining ones with the text. Mark the one answer that you think is correct.

Task 2: Examine the same part of the text again. What does it say about the influence of the teacher? Choose a sentence that clearly shows why your answer is the right one.

Task 3: Scan the first part of the text for the words 'school year'. When you have found them, read the sentence closely: what does it say about the number of interracial friendships? Don't forget to write down the line number(s) and the first and last words of the sentence.

Task 4: Scan for words like 'adolescence' and 'likely'. What does the text say about young teens entering adolescence: are they *more* or *less* likely to choose friends from a different ethnic background?

Task 5: You may find that all five sentence completions sound 'correct'. Don't forget that 'true' in tests like this means *true according to the text* (and not *true in general*). Which two of the five answers express ideas that can be found in similar form in the text? These are the answers you should mark.

Task 6: Examine the section of the text closely where Jennifer Orr talks about her oldest daughter. Did her daughter have only non-white friends at elementary school, only white friends, or a mix of both? Which of the answers are false? Which one can be proven true by comparison with the text?

Task 7: What does Jennifer Orr say about the parents' role with regard to interracial friendships? Complete the sentence in ca. 5–8 words.

Task 8: The task asks you to name two measures. The final paragraph of the text contains three sentences. Which of these name concrete measures? What is the function of the other sentence? Now write down the two measures in a few words each.

Solutions:

1 C (*'signaling … a world free of interpersonal racism'*, ll. 6–7)

3 FALSE. Evidence: *'teacher behaviors may … of interracial friendships.'* (ll. 11–12)

3 TRUE. Evidence: *'The study, led … cross-racial friendships decreases.'* (ll. 12–16)

4 FALSE. Evidence: *'as young people … ethnic groups decreases.'* (ll. 23–25)
5 B. Evidence: *'children of all backgrounds … and ethnicities.'* (ll. 26–28)
D. Evidence: *'a racially integrated student body … harmful stereotypes and bias.'* (ll. 31–33)
6 C. *'a highly diverse school … "Her close circle [of friends] included a Korean girl, a few Latino girls and boys, and at least one girl from the Middle East"'*, ll. 50–53)
7 Orr thinks that parents also *influence their children's friendships*. (*'The immediate thing that came to my mind … was how much parents may play a role'*, ll. 56–57. Other answers that say the same thing using different words are also correct.)
8 A. Mixed-race groups for class projects (*'When assigning class projects she encouraged diverse groupings of fourth- and fifth-graders to solidify existing friendships'*, ll. 63–64)
B Reading literature with examples of interracial friendships (*'Orr also turned to literature, using books with interracial friendships "to help kids see these friendships as normal and good."'*, ll. 66–68)

Part B: Writing

Task 1: The task requires you to compare two distinct situations: the ideal situation described in Anderson's article and the real situation described in the novel. Begin by writing down the most important aspects that foster the development of interracial friendships as named in the article:

- a diverse student body
- a classroom climate in which cross-racial friendships can grow and develop
- teachers who convey to their students the feeling that they are taken seriously and who strengthen their students' self-esteem.

Now make notes on the situation at Larry's middle school in Chabot:

- racial imbalance (overwhelming majority of black students)
- climate of intolerance and antagonism between the races (racist jokes, bullying)
- teachers (black women) only interested in injustice toward black girls, ignore Larry's plight

- teachers don't take their job seriously (teacher leaves the room for a smoke, although there was a racist incident in her class only minutes earlier; she makes no attempt to mediate in the conflict, but leaves it to the sixth-graders to settle their differences)

The third step is to draw conclusions from the material you have collected:

- The student body in Chabot is mixed, but not diverse; there are only two groups, the black majority and the white minority.
- The climate is such that interracial friendships are out of the question; the only contact between the two groups consists of racial insults and occasional violence.
- The teachers do nothing to create a climate of trust and openness; they are partial in their judgements and do not take their supervisory duty seriously.
- Under such conditions, interracial friendships cannot form, and if they did, they would not survive.

Task 2: You are free to support or to take issue with Jennifer Orr's belief, but in either case, you must name arguments to back up your view. For example, you could point out that readers in general (and especially young readers) can gain valuable knowledge of human nature from literature without actually experiencing the situations depicted in works of fiction. Or you could object that fictional representations of interracial friendship are often idealized and thus not a realistic model for real life.

You must also refer to the novel *Crooked Letter, Crooked Letter* as an example of a literary representation of interracial friendship. Here are two possible lines of argumentation with regard to the novel:

(positive)

- The novel shows that in spite of human failings and misunderstandings friendship between the races is possible.
- Main example: Larry and Silas
    - become friends until the outside world discovers and destroys their friendship;
    - 25 years later, Silas overcomes his moral turpitude and reaches out to Larry;

  - symbolism of brotherhood: 'all sons of one Father'.
- Other examples in the novel: in the Deep South of the early 21st century black and white people work side by side (e.g. Silas and French), race plays no role.
- The example of Silas and Larry, who must overcome great difficulties to re-establish their relationship, shows that even under difficult circumstances interracial friendship can flourish if both sides are willing.

(negative)
- The novel doesn't convincingly portray interracial friendship:
  - The boyhood friendship between Larry and Silas is very one-sided and would have ended by itself even if their father hadn't intervened;
  - The ending of the novel doesn't portray a thriving interracial friendship, only the acts of kindness that Angie and Silas perform before Larry's release;
  - We don't know if a real friendship will develop between the half-brothers;
  - Even if relations between black and white are more relaxed in the present than they were in the past, the races still live largely segregated lives:
    - Silas has social contacts mostly with other black people (Angie, Marla, Olivia); white friends are not mentioned in the novel;
    - Whites also tend to socialize with other whites (Larry, Stringfellow, Evelyn, Irina).
- The overall impression left by the novel is that relations between black and white (especially in the USA) suffer from the burden of the (racist) past and are thus fraught with tension.

Bildquellen
Cover: VISUM/Alfred Buellesbach; S. 6: INTERTOPICS/Empics/David Jensen; S. 11: Fotolia/Terence Mendoza; S. 12: Allstar/Dimension Films; S. 15: Fotolia/Sheri Armstrong; S. 17: Fotolia/EyeMark; S. 19: shutterstock/Scharfsinn; S. 24: moodboard/F1online; S. 27: mauritius images/alamy stock photo/Prisma by Dukas Presseagentur GmbH; S. 32: ddp images; S. 35: shutterstock/pixelheadphoto digitalskillet; S. 40: shutterstock/Sanit Fuangnakhon; S. 60: shutterstock/TFoxFoto; S. 81: akg / North Wind Picture Archives; S. 83: mauritius images/Circa Images/Glasshouse; S. 84: Action Press/Courtesy Everett Collection